C000263392

SHOW NO FEAR

SHOW NO FEAR

Bill Carson

ATHENA PRESS
LONDON

SHOW NO FEAR

ISBN 1 84401 532 7

First Published 2005 by
ATHENA PRESS
Queen's House, 2 Holly Road
Twickenham TW1 4EG
United Kingdom

Printed for Athena Press

PREFACE

I had no real desire to write a book; in fact it was something that I had never really thought about. I worked as a night-club bouncer for just over four years and in that time I had been involved in numerous altercations, sometimes there were amusing situations but most were not. I began by making a record of the more unusual and violent incidents that occurred and put them into a diary. After four years I had accumulated quite a lot of material. So I decided to put it all together; the result is what you read here.

I would not recommend this type of work to anyone; it was downright dangerous at times and your efforts go unnoticed and unappreciated most of the time. Throughout this book I make reference to ways in which I employed specific techniques in certain situations. I am not suggesting that this is the way you should conduct yourself if you are employed in a similar role. That was my way of dealing with 'situations'. Right or wrong I just did what I thought was necessary at the time either through fear, frustration or sometimes in anger. It is an honest account with a no holds barred approach and no punches are pulled. This book should not be used as a guide, it was not intended to be one; it is just an account of what happened while I was working in this dangerous occupation.

However having said that, you may find something of what I have written helpful to you when you're standing alone out there against the bad guys.

RIGHT HOOK

LEFT HOOK

WITH THANKS...

...to www.grafiklounge.com for the original cover design and photographs.

CONTENTS

INTO THE UNKNOWN

September 1993... Pete and I had been working together for a number of years.

He, like myself, was into martial arts and keeping fit; both of us used to work the night shift one week out of every two, which threw your usual training routine out of sync. One night we decided to set up a makeshift gym in one of the disused garages which was part of the building complex we worked in. We would train at around two in the morning for about three-quarters of an hour during one of our extended breaks, much to the annoyance of some of the old gits who were trying to get their heads down in the building next door.

Our wages at that time were less than two hundred a week. After one of our early morning training sessions we began to discuss ways in which we might be able to supplement our income, and after thinking about it for a couple of days we had decided to put our physical prowess, charm and boyish good looks to some use.

What we eventually decided upon was putting ourselves up for hire as security for private parties and functions. It was now full steam ahead into our new career move. The word went around and after a while we were hired.

And so our very first night on the door: it was a favour really for some guy who we worked with. He was arranging an eighteenth birthday party for his daughter and was concerned about things possibly being ruined by gatecrashers.

The venue was a local cricket club. It was to run from eight until twelve and was by invitation only, which made life a bit easier for us. He paid us up front, I think it was thirty quid each. So far so good.

We didn't really know what to expect, this being our first night, but we had worked on a few things just in case it all went pear-shaped. Our philosophy was that we would treat people the way we would like to be treated ourselves and anyone who gave us any attitude problems would get zero tolerance. The important thing to remember is that no matter what, we were going home in one piece. We put a great deal of thought and energy into finding the best ways in which we could eject troublemakers quickly and with as little fuss as possible. Not an easy thing to achieve. I had studied a lot of restraining techniques from the karate and judo manuals that I had accumulated over the years. My search through the numerous books led me to find a manual that I had completely forgotten about; it was called *All in Fighting*. In fact it was a Second World War unarmed combat instruction booklet, which had some very interesting techniques inside. Research on the subject led us to discover a total immobilization strangle and choke hold. It was a dangerous technique and must be used with caution; what I mean is if you were to lock the hold on for too long or with too much pressure on the person's neck it would without doubt cause a serious injury. The beauty of it was though, that once you had performed it correctly there is virtually no way out of it; giving you complete control over the transgressor. Also with a minor adjustment it is possible to dislocate the neck, that's why it has to be practised over and over in order for it to be used effectively without causing injury. I consider myself to be very proficient with this particular method of restraint and over the years I've used it dozens of times (when necessary) without any problems.

The only problem with continuously practising these strangleholds was the wear and tear on the neck and throat area; we both had sore necks for a month.

The only way to find out how effective your strangleholds and arm locks are is to execute them on your training partner and vice versa. That way you get to know how much force is required to get the desired effect, that is, compliance.

I picked Pete up at half seven, he jumped into the motor and we headed west into unknown territory.

We arrived at the venue at about ten to eight; it was a beautiful summer evening. As we pulled into the car park a cool summer breeze greeted us. We made our way along the narrow straight path, which led us up to the cricket pavilion, and once inside a short, fat barman called us over to the bar.

'Are you two looking after the door for us tonight then?'

With that he produced two bottles of lager from the cold shelf. We thanked him for the beers and had a walk around the place. It was a rectangular shaped sports hall and at one end people were busying themselves setting up the bar and at the other end the DJ was plugging in his speakers and testing the microphone: 'Testing, testing, one, two, three, screeeeeeeeeeeeech!'

Pete was savouring the last drops of his beer with a broad grin; I have heard that he likes the occasional drink. We take up our positions either side of the door, black suit, white shirt, very smart. The family has just arrived and after a brief introduction the rest of the guests start to file past, each producing an invitation.

There must be about a hundred or so in now. One

woman, who was of rapidly advancing years shall we say, kept looking over in Pete's direction; she approaches him and whispers in his ear.

'You're a big boy, are you big all over?'

I turn to Pete as she walks away and say, 'You can't half pick them, mate.'

She looked like Vera Duckworth on a bad night.

I spoke too soon: she came over to me next. At the same time this other old trout was dancing provocatively in front of Pete; she was gyrating her very large backside in his direction. Every now and then she would lift up the front of her dress exposing her enormous thighs, she was like a young elephant jumping about. Once around her would be twice around the gas works. Everyone was having a really good time as the party got into full swing; we had no trouble of any serious nature to deal with. The only problem we had was trying to hide ourselves from the over-amorous attentions of two old grannies. I don't think they had a full set of teeth between them.

'When are you two going to take us out for a drink then?' One of them asks, winking at me with one of her mascara-encrusted eyes.

I whisper to Pete: 'They must have turned up on the wrong night, grab a granny night is next week.'

'I bet your one's flattened a bit of grass in her time,' Pete says.

The only real irritating aspect of the night was the DJ; he kept coming over to us and saying he's done door work before and he's a kick boxer and so on, and not to worry because he will steam in good style if it kicks off... He wouldn't have been able to knock the skin off of a rice pudding.

The evening passed with relative ease, actually it was

quite a pleasant occasion. We made our escape through one of the rear fire exits to evade our two antiquated groupies who were loitering with intent at the main entrance. A quick sprint across the car park and into the little Renault 5. I point the car in the direction of the A4 and home.

The next day we were at our regular place of work when the guy who we had done the security for the previous evening comes over to thank us. He was very happy with the way the evening had gone and the way we had conducted ourselves. He goes on to say that after we had left the venue the DJ had been involved in a fight. He had received a right-hander from a drunken old Pakistani bloke who had wandered into the cricket ground and found his way into the back of the DJ's van. The first of many nights on the door was a good one.

A few weeks had passed since our debut; we decided to have some business cards printed and Pete drafted a superb letter explaining our services. We would go for a bit of a mooch around the pubs and clubs in our local area and have a butchers at the door staff to see how they shaped up. If they were a bit scruffy or looked like a couple of wallies we would put the place on our mailing list and send the manager our details.

We had received a few replies but they were not offering the right money. An extra few quid was the sole reason why we have decided to enter into this line of work, we were not going to work for peanuts.

I want to explain that we are not hard men and don't want to be, we also have nothing to prove to anyone either. I think we are entering into this with the right kind of attitude, we're no mugs though. You have a pop at us and you will pay dearly.

The next job finally arrived, it was through a friend of a

friend, we were being asked to work the door at a private party in Chelsea.

The money and the hours had been agreed, a quick change into our black suits, switch on, and we set off for West London.

We decided to take the tube, because the parking in this area was a nightmare and with the traffic at this time in the evening it would have taken us ages to get there.

We were greeted by a steady pelting of heavy rain as we left the station; we quickly made our way through the long, wet, narrow high street, which eventually led us to the corner of the road. A right turn and three doors down we arrived.

Just as I was about to ring the bell the door opened and inside the hallway was Philip: he was of medium height with grey thinning hair and quite small in stature.

'Hello, boys, I've been expecting you.'

'Fucking hell, keep your hand on your ha'penny, Pete.'

We stood in the hallway and he asks if we would like our money now or at the end.

'I think now would be fine, thanks.'

'How much did we agree?'

'Forty-five each.'

With that he pulls a wad of notes out from his pocket; he must have had at least a grand there.

'Well, here's fifty each. Come over here and have a drink.'

We follow him into the main room of the apartment; in the corner was a large plastic dustbin full of ice cubes and bottles of lager; he knocks the tops off two bottles and hands us one each. Over to our left was a large fireplace with a blazing log fire in it; we stood in front of it for a while and dried ourselves off.

On the other side of the room was a huge dining table, about a third of it was covered in champagne glasses. At the end of the table were two dozen bottles of the very best bubbly. Philip turns towards us and says, 'What I want you to do is enjoy yourselves and just imagine you are guests. The main reason I wanted you here is that a couple of the people I'm expecting can get a little boisterous after a few drinks, but I'm sure they will behave once they know that I have you two boys around.'

We were asked to go down to the basement; Philip says he'll come and get us if anything happens. Basically we were to stay down there until he gives us a shout.

We were led down a flight of stairs and into the basement, which was quite large, about twenty-foot square and right in the middle was a pool table. We had a few games and after about half an hour Philip comes down to introduce us to one of his friends; his name was Johnny, the Earl of something, a right eccentric character. He was tall, thin with dark shoulder-length hair, he was already pissed and obviously on something.

That was confirmed when he asked us if we wanted any 'gear'; he opened his jacket pocket and inside he had a substantial amount of pills and tablets in a variety of colours. Thanks but no thanks, not interested, mate. I don't know what they were but I would imagine that after a couple of those you would be floating around the ceiling like a mushroom. Mind-bending drugs are not our scene.

The place was getting jam-packed. The majority of the people who showed up all spoke with that plumb in the mouth acquired accent, the upper classes' old boy, jolly good show, and all that, what, what. You know the kind with that certain type of attitude, with an outward show of superiority. After a few drinks and a go of whatever else was on offer the masks soon began to slip exposing their true personalities; they then became just like any other annoying drunk.

The two of us were fast becoming a bit of a curiosity; the guests were coming down to the basement just to have a look at the 'bouncers' especially the women, who were poking their heads around the doorway giggling childishly and pointing in our direction.

A group of young women were all moving rhythmically to the latest dance music surrounded by Hooray Henrys who were all studying the form and guzzling champagne like it was going out of fashion. The women outnumbered the men by at least two to one and the basement was definitely becoming the place to be. It was getting packed and a little rowdy as Johnny came running in to where we were, glass of champagne in one hand, spliff in the other and says at the top of his voice:

'You won't get any trouble, lads, just a few Sloane Rangers running around going yar! Yar! Yar'!

Strange man.

It was getting far too crowded for us in the basement, the air being filled with the distinctive smell of weed. We decide to go upstairs where we could breathe a little easier. We stood at the back of the main room either side of the large table, which was full of drinks and clean empty glasses; an attractive middle-aged woman approached Pete and engaged him in conversation, he thought she was coming over to chat him up. What she actually said to him was that she would like two glasses of champagne and a bottle of lager. He had decided to wear a bow tie for this particular function and was mistaken for the waiter; I had to laugh as the bow tie came off in a flash.

There was lots of bedroom activity; if the bedrooms

were full they would be mooching about in the dark corners of the large conservatory.

At about midnight Philip came over to us and said that the two guys who he thought were going to cause trouble had now left and that we were no longer on duty.

'Stay for the rest of the party as my guests if you like, boys, or you can leave now if you prefer.'

Our job was done so we decided not to hang around; if we were quick we would just be able to catch the last tube home. Philip could not thank us enough.

'Thank you very much, lads, I was so glad you were here.'

On our way out I gave him one of our business cards.

'Oh that's fucking neat... Good night, lads.'

As we were about to leave one of the guests jumps out in front of us barring our way to the front door.

'I want to take a picture of these two; they are the fucking stars of the party. Hic!'

Philip suggested he didn't take the photo and to step aside, he wasn't sure how we were going to react.

'These people are the fucking stars; I want a picture of them. Burp!'

Philip interjects again and says these people duff people up for a living so get out of the way.

The door closed and we made our way through the cold wet streets, arriving at the underground station with a few minutes to spare before the last train arrived. We boarded the train quite content with the evening's outcome. It was a good night with no trouble at all, a couple of beers and a pizza, plus fifty quid each resting very happily in our pockets.

We were hooked and hungry for more.

Throughout the journey home a pissed up Aussie had

been casting the occasional glance over in our direction.

He eventually says, ‘Are you two bouncers, then?’

He was referring to our black attire.

‘No we’re with the Royal Philharmonic… fuck off,’ was my reply.

FIGHTING FIT

It's been a few weeks since our last engagement, we change the business cards and basically blitzkrieg the pubs and clubs with them. This was all before the new strict licensing laws that are now in place, so in those days we were a bit of a law unto ourselves. Nowadays every door supervisor has to obtain a licence from the council at some considerable cost and attend a two-day course as well which deals with first aid, fire fighting, and the understanding of the licensing laws, powers of arrest and the use of reasonable force. I could go on but it's getting boring.

We were not getting a very good response to our cards and letters; a few follow-up phone calls were made. I rang the manager of the first pub we had sent one of our letters to and asked for the name and number of the security company that they were using.

Basically our idea was to find out if any of these pubs and clubs were unhappy with their security arrangements. If they were, we would offer our services. But virtually every place we contacted we kept hearing the same company name. It looked like this little firm had most if not all of the contracts in the area.

Well, so I suppose if you can't beat them join them. After having a chat with Pete we decided to give them a ring. A fella with a Scots accent answered the phone.

'Do you have any door supervisor positions available at the moment?'

'Have you done any of this kind of work before?'

'I've done a bit, and a mate of mine is also looking for some work.'

'Right then you had better come down and see me for an interview.'

We arranged a suitable time; it was for three o'clock on the following Thursday.

We had to bring with us two passport-size photos (the worst I have ever seen) and also any relevant background information.

The office was located in the basement of a large restaurant; there was a small staircase leading down to the entrance. I pressed the intercom and announced our arrival. I didn't get a reply but after a few seconds we heard the sound of the locks being released.

Clank! Clank! Crunch! Clonk!

A very large individual who had a shaven square-shaped head finally opened the door; all that was missing was the bolt through his neck. We were then invited in; he didn't ask us in, he just beckoned us forward. There was a fella sitting behind a desk inside another smaller office over to our left. He looked up and stopped what he was doing.

'Take a seat, lads, I'll be with you shortly,' he said.

I had a quick glance around the office; it was obviously a company in its infancy, quite a dingy place with no ceiling just the exposed floor joists of the restaurant above. Nothing on the floor just the bare concrete. At the other end of the office was a desk, which was covered in papers. On the wall was a large noticeboard with the names of all the venues they were looking after, cross-referenced with the people who were looking after them. The guy behind the desk introduced himself to us with a firm handshake.

'Hello, boys, how are you doing? My name is John.'

He then asks us if we have our photos for our ID badges.

'Yes, and the background information you asked for.'

He has a brief look at our CVs and remarks: 'Peter and Paul – the two saints?'

'Well, we're good boys… But not that good.'

We stayed and chatted for a while, and after about twenty minutes John says that he will contact us in a few days. He seemed decent enough; I am a pretty good judge of character usually, he seemed like a very genuine sort of bloke. He gave the impression that you wouldn't want to get on the wrong side of him though. I also got the feeling that there was definitely more to these people than meets the eye. We will see how it goes.

As we were leaving I notice a door that was slightly ajar. They had turned one of the empty offices into a gym complete with punch bags and various other pieces of training equipment; we couldn't resist the temptation. Pete held the bag and I threw a few boxing combinations at it.

I have always done some sort of training. I first studied karate back in the seventies; I think it was the summer of 1973. I must have been about fourteen at the time.

The karate club was only a short walk from my house, no more than half a mile away. The first I knew of the club's existence was when I saw a friend of mine walking through the park. I was playing football at the time.

I asked him where he was going, 'Karate,' he said. That sounds interesting, I thought.

He explained that some fella had given him a good hiding. Revenge being his initial motivation he decided to learn how to fight so that if he ever saw the guy again he could dispatch him with a few well-aimed karate chops.

Hang on, mate; I'll come with you I say to him. I wanted to have a look at some of this karate stuff, some of the other lads decided to tag along as well.

Once inside the club we witnessed some strange activities taking place. People bowing to each other and everyone running about in white pyjamas. As the instructor walked in everyone got into their positions.

The other lads who came to watch were all taking the piss and went after a while. But I stayed right to the end. I thought it was brilliant.

I joined up as soon as I could, and never looked back. I have been involved in the martial arts ever since. I didn't have a great deal of confidence when I was a kid; I would run home if someone was picking on me. One reason that some people decide to run away instead of standing their ground to fight is through lack of knowledge. You don't know what to do so you make a run for it. Karate made the difference: that is where I would find the knowledge therefore dispelling my fears. It gave me the confidence that I thought I'd never have. I stayed at the club for many years and had some unforgettable superb training sessions.

THE AUTHOR AND OTHER KARATE PRACTITIONERS BEFORE A DEMONSTRATION, LATE 1970S

Fear is met by courage and destroyed.

Saturday mornings were without a doubt the best: we called it 'animal hour'.

We would assemble in two lines one behind the other, the command would go out, take your Gi* tops off front line, turn around and face your partner.

Twenty punches into your partner's stomach hard and fast, press-ups, sit-ups, squats, and then a run through the streets in bare feet. After that the free sparring would begin (more like free for all;) the only protection we wore was a groin guard. I remember getting changed after one session, I took off my groin guard and examined the plastic protective cup, it was completely smashed in two... Everything else was intact, thank God.

That's what it was like in those days; the next week I fractured someone's ribs with a reverse punch. You would come out of there with bruises all over you. There was this guy, I can't remember his name, but I nicknamed him hiza (hiza being the Japanese word for the knee). The only technique he seemed to possess was the knee strike.

He would grab hold of you and try to knee you in the knackers. Once or twice you might be able to avoid, but a full three-minute assault on your cobblers and he's bound to hit the target a least once. The techniques we practised were mainly geared for the 'knock down' fighting which was exactly as it sounds, knock your opponent down with full contact blows to the body to win basically. The training required was extremely tough, it was definitely the hardest training I have ever experienced. Mind you it's up to you how hard you want to train; if you put nothing in you'll get nothing out. Hand conditioning was something that was

---

* Gi: the jacket worn by karate practitioners.

practised regularly as well, by the more dedicated of us. Just to explain about the hand conditioning. It is very prevalent in some karate schools and non-existent in others. A punching drill required you to repeatedly strike with full power into a small woven straw punching pad (*makiwara*) that was attached to a four inch by four inch five-foot-high wooden post. This would toughen the impact area of the fist; the striking area should be the index finger and second finger knuckles, 70% emphasis on the index finger knuckle and 30% on the second finger knuckle. It would also teach you how to punch correctly because if you hit it wrong you would know about it. It takes years and years of dedicated unending practise to perfect these karate strikes. I used to practise on the punching post a great deal; I even put one up in my back garden. Also all press-ups were performed on your knuckles using pieces of flat pinewood board.

This type of training is only practised in the toughest of karate schools. For your first dan *(black belt)* for example you had to have fifty consecutive fights. It was full contact and no gloves were worn, kicking to the groin was out, also punching to the head was against the rules. Thigh kicks were my speciality, if you delivered one in the right place the fight would be over. I received a kick in the thigh in one match that was so hard that the bruising came out on the opposite side of my leg. It took me a week to shake off the pain and walk properly. Another knockdown fight I remember was when I had been struck with a spinning back kick; the guy's heel struck me with full power to the side of the head. I dropped down on to one knee, I didn't feel any pain but what did happen was that I saw a group of perfectly formed five-pointed little stars spinning slowly in front of me. I used to think that was something that you only saw in cartoons. Take it from it me it actually does happen. I got back up to get in a few good blows of my own. I had a black and blue ear for a couple of weeks after though.

You have to learn to take it before you can dish it out.

Every winter we were invited to take part in a Japanese-style training course; it was held in the grounds of a large private school in Buckinghamshire.

The school had vast grounds, where we would all be running around in the mud, rain and snow. Sparring matches were organised in the fields where we also took part in the roughest game of British bulldog you have ever seen: flying kicks and elbow strikes were traded with equal enthusiasm.

But the best part of the course was saved till the end. In the grounds they had a large waterfall, each person would go into the stream and under the waterfall to execute fifty karate punches with the heavy steady flow of ice cold water cascading down onto you. Afterwards we were all invited to the local pub where chicken and chips in a basket were laid on washed down with a couple of well deserved pints. I'll never forget those Saturday morning training sessions with Frank, Tony, Nigel, Kevin, Keith, Eddie, Martin and Bill, and everyone else who used to train at that Dojo in the mid seventies and eighties.

Frank would join us sometimes at the local pub after training and one evening he began to talk about a book. The book was called *A Book of Five Rings*, written in sixteen forty five by the Samurai warrior, Miyamoto Musashi, who by the time he was thirty had fought and killed more than sixty men. Believing he was invincible he retired to a cave and wrote his book. The book is about fighting strategy, but there is more to it than that, it has taken me years to understand some of what he has written. It is a superb book and is a constant source of inspiration. I advise any serious martial artist to obtain a copy.

Frank was now expanding his empire and lessons with him were becoming fewer and fewer unfortunately, because he is without a doubt one of the best… Ouss!

The final straw for me came when a guy who had been at the club for a couple of years was taking the karate lesson and he decided to omit the usual sparring session. Karate without our usual *kumite,* what was the world coming to?

This was unfortunately becoming a regular occurrence, no Frank, and no sparring; sadly I decided to leave the karate school. I had been training there for about eight years; I had become very proficient at karate and had built up a strong mental and physical toughness that has served me well over the years. I must admit I did miss the old place for a while. I decided to build my own dojo (gym), in my back garden where we would be free to practise the way we wanted to and do as much sparring as we liked.

I suppose every cloud has its silver lining; if I had stayed at the club the back garden gym would not have been built. I contacted a garage manufacturer who built the thing around my own design. Eventually I settled on it being fifteen feet in length and ten feet wide. It had to be built high enough for the punch bags, which were suspended from the thickest beam I could find, eight inches in depth by six inches wide by ten foot in length. When it was all bolted together it looked absolutely superb. Now that I had built the thing we needed to buy some equipment to put in it. We used to go to a place along the Fulham Palace Road which is sadly no longer there any more. It had everything you needed to equip a boxing gym. Andy, a mate of mine, drove Pete and myself down there to get the equipment. The only problem was that Andy had turned up in a green Citroën 2CV. It looked like a cross between a frog and a small green house on wheels. Not exactly designed for heavy weights either; we went around one corner on two wheels; I thought the thing was going over. It got us there and back though... just about. I took the tube the next time.

The security company contacted me and said that they were willing to take the both of us on but on a trial basis at first. They said that we would be contacted in a few days with the details of our first assignment.

We had now joined the ranks of the professionals.

This called for a complete restructuring of our training routine. A new one would have to be designed in order to get ourselves into fighting fit shape.

A ten-minute warm up. Stretching, calisthenics.

Three minutes of skipping. For three rounds.

Three hundred press-ups in sets of fifty.

Six hundred sit-ups in sets of two hundred.

Left and right hooks non-stop on the heavy bag. For three rounds.

Combination punching on the heavy bag 1-minute non-stop. 5 times each.

After that some sparring matches and then to finish off we practised our unarmed combat techniques. We trained like that four times a week, every week.

I felt that this was enough to get us into good condition, hard training without knocking your pipe out completely. We were now ready for anything.

We had a regular little crew who used to turn up: Tony, Pete and my old mates from my school, Peter, Andy and John. Tony was the smallest and lightest of the lads but pound for pound the strongest. He trained like a demon and was as hard as nails. Pete was six two and seventeen and a half stones and always trained very hard and had perfected an excellent left jab, one of the best I've seen (and felt). Peter, my other mate, whom I have known since I was at school was the biggest and the heaviest of us at over eighteen stone and a touch over six two. He presented a formidable opponent. Initially he trained for many years in Kung Fu but adapted to boxing very well; I think I've still got a lump under my chin to prove it. Andy was the new boy weighing in at eleven stone and with no previous experience. He had to start from scratch, but was a fast learner and very game, he also never pulled a punch. He would try and knock your block off every time, which was good in a way, because it kept you on your toes – in one match Andy received a really hard blow from Peter which resulted in a broken rib. I think it's called learning the hard way; he healed up pretty quick and was back training about a month later, a little bit wiser. And John who is a professional doorman and the only one still training with me today, at fifteen and half stones and six foot, strong, fast and determined and has a very potent right-hand punch. And last but not least myself, at six foot and sixteen stones I considered myself to be a good all-rounder in the fistic arts. You know about my martial arts background but the boxing was something that came naturally to me. I studied a great deal of fight film; the fighters I used to watch most were Joe Louis and Rocky Marciano. Joe Louis was one of the best combination punchers ever and reigned for eleven years as the heavyweight champion of the world. Rocky Marciano has got to be the toughest of all time and with his murderous right-hand punch was never beaten. He had forty-nine fights, forty-nine wins with forty-three knockouts. He has remained the only world heavyweight champion in history to retire undefeated. These are the guys I would study to see how they delivered their punches and how they got themselves into position to unleash their devastating attacks. I also studied a fighter called Jack Dempsey from the 1920s; his fight against the giant Jess Willard for the world heavyweight title was one of the most brutal ever to be shown on film. So with the Joe Louis combinations and with Rocky Marciano's right hander with a bit of Jack Dempsey thrown in for good measure I set about adopting their techniques and incorporating them into our training routines.

We trained hard, still using the training schedule: press-ups, sit-ups, bag work and skipping being the fundamental building blocks. The sparring at the end of each session was as tough as I could make it. I felt it had to be made as real as possible. Quite a few schools that teach martial arts for example don't ever get anywhere near the kind of realism that you need for an actual encounter with someone. The person who has been training at a school that teaches a semi- or a non-contact type of sparring is going to get battered big time in the real world. I call it the fantasy island syndrome.

Once a week we decided that one of us would stay up and fight for ten three-minute rounds; it was a great test of stamina, strength and spirit. One sparring match which springs to mind was with Pete; as usual it would start off relatively normal and gather momentum as it continued. Tony was doing the time keeping, two rounds gone and Pete was fighting really hard with absolutely no quarter given and none taken. The third round had started when Pete caught me with a superb left jab followed by another left into the rib cage, quickly followed by two more left jabs to the head. It put me on the defensive and I started to go backwards, but my training determination and spirit kept me going. If you get caught in the solar plexus or floating ribs there's nothing you can do but cover up and weather the storm.

I was in the corner and under attack from Peter's persistent left-hand jabs; I lured him in and waited for the right moment to counter attack. I threw a fast left hand followed by a right cross-combined with a hard left uppercut to the jaw followed by a rib crunching right hand to the body. It sent Pete crashing through the door of the gym and out into the back garden where the fighting continued, much to the surprise of the builders who were putting in some double glazing next door. Two of them turned around quickly to see what was going on and one of them almost fell off the scaffolding.

At that point Tony calls a halt to the proceedings. Pete commented afterwards that when the upper cut landed on his chin he thought he saw the sun and the moon rise simultaneously and that it was only sheer bloody mindedness and a refusal to give in that made him carry on. (I call it spirit.) You've got to be able to take it in the gym. If you can't you will be in a lot of trouble in a real street fight. The lads came in all shapes and sizes so one round you would be fighting someone who was six two; the next round you would be fighting someone shorter and faster. Which was good because in a real fight you can't pick and choose your opponent. It was all done with the right kind of attitude and with absolutely no malice, in fact quite the opposite. We had some right old punch ups in there. Believe it or not it was all extremely enjoyable. You have to take part in it to understand what I mean; we were all very fit and strong and could take the punishment. A great confidence builder as well. The sparring was also intended to remove the fear of fighting. Basically we were not afraid of taking a few and so if you can remove that fear and accept the fact that you may have to take a clump or two, violent confrontations are slightly easier to handle.

Andy died recently; he was just into his late thirties. I have been thinking about him a lot during the writing of this book, what a waste. He was a troubled character who found it difficult to handle the real world. We both shared a common interest in art, drawing and sketching etc; I remember going up to the Tate Gallery with him and studying all the great works of art. Sadly we won't be able to make those trips any more. We had some good laughs with Andy, he really was a likeable man. I did my best to help him when he was in trouble and I know that my efforts where appreciated by him. He is remembered with great affection by me, my family and friends. We drifted apart over the last few years and only bumped into one another very occasionally. I had received my usual Christmas card from him and then found out that four months later he was dead.

He was cremated and his ashes taken away by his family.

Strange, isn't it? Only when someone is no longer around do you begin to realise what you really thought of them. *Wish you were here mate*... Life goes on.

Back to the door work. John phoned and asked if Peter and I would like to work Saturday night.

'OK, mate, where do want us to go?'

He gave me the location and I asked my usual question. 'What's the money like?'

'How does £90 a piece sound?'

'Sounds fine, mate, we will be there.'

'You will have to be there from 10 p.m. till about 8 a.m.'

Kings Cross was our destination. We boarded the train and left the leafy suburbs of Ealing behind and after about forty-five minutes we arrive at Kings Cross. Grey and uninviting, a run-down inner city dump where every vice imaginable was on offer.

As we exit the station the police are everywhere. Six coppers are trying to arrest some black guy who is brandishing a large carving knife and is taunting them with it; it took them ages to deal with the situation. We were tempted to go over and show them how it should be done. Mind you they would have probably nicked *us* for being to rough with the gentleman.

Eventually they all jump on him and then he is very gently placed in the back of the police van. I thought that they were far too hesitant with the guy; anyone who carries a weapon of that nature and then decides to use it should get absolutely no mercy. I have no idea what sort of training the police receive with regards to tackling situations of this nature. It all looked very amateurish and haphazard from where we were standing and a lot of luck was involved. He will probably get some tea and biscuits and a slap on the wrist when they get him back to the station.

A good start to the evening...

We arrived at our destination about half an hour too early and so we set off in search of the nearest battle cruiser.

We find a pub close to the venue, it had a few hell's angels mooching about inside but they didn't take much notice of us. The music was excellent. As we walked in the jukebox was playing one of my favourite pieces of heavy rock music, *Paranoid* by Black Sabbath. Two halves of lager later and it was time to shoot over the road.

The venue was and still is a very popular place: three massive warehouses linked together with enough room for thousands of revellers.

As we enter the venue John was standing in the main entrance.

'You made it then.'

'Hello, mate what's happening?'

'You two come with me.'

We followed him down a flight of stairs through a long corridor, to where we were to spend the majority of the night. The two of us were introduced to the other member of the company who jointly runs it with John.

'All right, lads, if you'd just like to listen in.'

He then proceeded to show us how to search someone for any drugs or weapons etc.

Firstly everyone must be searched without exception, ask them if they have any needles on them, search their hats, boots, bags, everything. The underneath of the collar on the shirt or jacket is one of the favourite hiding places for small amounts of drugs.

He then proceeded to demonstrate the search on one of the staff. Start at the top and work down, tell them to raise their arms, feel down each sleeve, ask them to remove any head gear, then do the collar, and over the shoulders and around the back. Then grab hold of the waistband of the trousers and give them a good shake, you never know, something might fall out, then down the inside of the legs and then the outside and finally the boots; ask them to take them off if you feel it's necessary.

If we found any drugs they were all put into a steel drugs box which was taken to the local police station the next day.

A few minutes later the first of the night's revellers started to emerge.

We were stopping and searching the punters for a good couple of hours, we had most definitely drawn the short straw. Two huge queues were formed stretching right back to the high street: boys on the left and the girls over to the right-hand side. There were hundreds of scantily clad young females, scruffy looking dudes and undesirables of every description descending on the place.

A couple of old trannies were parading themselves up and down the never-ending ranks of impatient young people, dressed in over-elaborate costumes trying to amuse the punters who were having to wait forever to gain entry. The guy who had organised the event, who incidentally was dressed in a long flowing purple gown topped off with a witch's hat, was making himself very busy, flitting about in an excited fashion with an over the top foppish manner, giving orders left, right and centre with animated gestures like some kind of demented orchestral conductor.

Peter turns towards me as he was searching the lower half of some scruffy looking bastard; his face had the expression of someone who had just taken a bite out of a very bitter lemon.

'What's up, mate?'

Pete says, 'I'll tell you later.'

And so we eventually get a break, I say to Pete, 'What happened when you were searching that bloke?'

Pete goes on to explain that while he was searching around the back of the guy's trousers he had discovered that he had shit his pants…

Two things sprang to my mind: the first was that this fella is now going to be wandering around all night with his pants full of shite, secondly, Pete has just had his hand around the back of this bloke's trousers and is now munching away on a cheese and pickle sandwich using the same *unwashed* hand.

After our well-deserved break we were asked to patrol for the rest of the night. The sickly bittersweet smell of puff was inescapable. Whilst doing our rounds we observed some curious sights. Some individuals were very lively jigging about furiously on the same spot, head down, looking at the floor and some were just standing staring into space open mouthed with blank expressions and soaked in sweat. If that was their idea of a good night out they could keep it; they paid fifteen quid a piece to come here and do that. An evening out at the races or a dog meeting for a piss up with a few pals, that's my idea of a good night out.

It was absolutely boiling, someone must have turned the heating on full whack. The best little earner must have been the water concession; whoever had that must have made a fortune. At 6 a.m. the end was in sight, a twenty-five strong team of bouncers form ranks and herd the remnants of the crowd towards the main exit. The snatch squads had a busy night though, intercepting drugs and the people who deal in them. When they were caught they were given very rough treatment and literally kicked out.

We collected our cash and set off towards the station… and home.

I think we did that venue three or four times, I didn't like the place much, it had too many *bad vibes*. On one occasion a member of the security team was stabbed to death on the premises whilst trying to apprehend a drug dealer.

This can be a very dangerous profession; many doormen have been killed in the line of duty. It's a statistic that I feel will only sadly increase especially with today's growing gun and knife culture, and the willingness to commit these murders with very little, if any, provocation. When they are caught they are awarded a sentence that rarely befits the crime and they will probably only serve two thirds of it. With their defence lawyers bringing out the old chestnut 'he had a deprived childhood'; that's all bollocks as far as I'm concerned. These do-gooders who argue this way I feel have a lot to answer for. What we need are strong laws in place that protect the 'victims' and not the perpetrators. The other day it was reported in the newspaper that a young boy who was just out on an errand for his mother was stabbed to death for a mobile phone. Words cannot express how I feel about such things. If I had my way I would reintroduce the death penalty for such crimes. The taking of someone's life in a premeditated cold-blooded attack with a knife, that person has to pay the ultimate price, anything less than that and I feel that justice has not been served. Take away the knife and what are we left with? A pathetic coward. There's no margin for error with a knife, they are designed to kill. Unfortunately the reality is that these cold, sick 'people', for want of a better description, do exist and so we have to be ready to defend ourselves against them as best we can. If one of these types of individuals pulls a knife on me, my response will be a relentless unmerciful, devastating beating. I don't like people who carry knives. OK, I'll put my soap box away now.

We set about acquiring bullet and stab-proof vests and every knife self-defence manual I could lay my hands on. We studied and practised the techniques that seemed to be the most effective and uncomplicated and incorporated them into our training routine. We practised them over and over until they became second nature.

One of the most important things that we discovered while researching the subject of knife self-defence was the *seizing of the knife hand*, and not to let go of it. Literally hang on for dear life. Running away is always a good idea... if you think you can.

I have given some thought to putting together a practical self-defence manual in the near future. Not like some that you see with the use of flamboyant kicks and complicated blocking routines, they would probably get you killed if you tried to use them against someone who had a knife. My idea is to write a manual that deals with the reality of what is required to subdue your attacker so you can make your escape and survive the ordeal.

I have worn a covert kevlar vest ever since the incident at King's Cross; they are not cheap but an obvious essential piece of kit. I advise anyone involved in this type of occupation to obtain one. Another piece of kit we used to bring was a groin guard for obvious reasons and a pair of good quality leather gloves are always a good idea. I had the ones that were knife proof, they were ordinary leather gloves but with kevlar inserts. We always wore boots as opposed to shoes; the reason being is that they don't come off. Pete was going in to deal with a fight one night closely followed by me. I accidentally trod on the back of his shoe and it came flying off. He was hopping around in the dark for a good few minutes trying to find it. By the time he had retrieved it the situation had been dealt with.

Monday afternoon... I had just finished a particularly tough two-hour training session, and so I go through the usual routine; first a hot bath followed by something to eat and then I'd get my head down for a couple of hours, but my sleep was interrupted by some very loud knocking at my front door. I opened the door to find a guy who was trying to deliver some new kitchen equipment.

As I looked out and up the garden path his mate was coming down with it on a trolley. I have four steps leading down to my front door and he banged it down every one of them. As he gets to the front door I say to him if it doesn't work I'll know why.

'Don't worry about it, man, it's tightly packed,' was his reply.

They eventually bring the stuff through and I ask them if they could unpack it and also take the packaging with them. The driver had no problems with what I'd asked them to do but the other guy was moaning about it, he was a tall lean black fella. We're not supposed to do this, he was saying to the other guy who just carried on taking the packaging away. The other guy decided not to take any of the cardboard and started to walk out with a right strop on. As he walks past me he looks at me with a stupid half sneer.

'Have you got a problem, mate?' I say to him.

'No, you got the problem, man.'

As he turns around he tells me to fuck off.

Smack! A hard fast right-hand punch knocks him off the doorstep onto his back and into the plants in the front garden. I have never seen anyone more surprised; the look of absolute disbelief on his face was a picture. I think he was the type of person who rarely had anyone stand up to him let alone bounce a right hander off his chin. I'll not allow anyone to talk to me like that especially on my own doorstep.

As I go outside after him to finish him off he was just getting to his feet. He's in a crouched position leaning forward with his arms waving about in front of him as if he were in a fog. I close in on him and throw a left hook and right upper cut combination; they both missed the target. He must have felt the wind of the upper cut as it went past; it was millimetres away from hitting the target. I put so much power into the upper cut I lost my balance and fell backwards over the dustbin. Now he sees his opportunity, he basically falls on top off me and whacks me in the face with a big bunch of keys, which opens a cut over my right eye.

I could not get to my feet because the dustbin was under

my legs, bang! He's caught me again, but his blows lacked any real power. I think that the clump I had given him had taken away most off his strength.

I manage to get my foot into his stomach and boot him off; I try to get to my feet but that fucking dustbin is well and truly on his side. He comes for me again but this time as he comes toward me to deliver his attack I manage to catch him with a blow which opened a gash just under his eye; it unzipped like a purse and a fair amount of his claret began to flow. That gave me the chance to get to my feet; as I get up he does a runner and hurdles the front gate. I was willing to leave it at that but he decided to throw half a brick in my direction and run off. It missed and hit the window frame, which cracked the glass.

For the first time during the whole encounter I completely lost my temper; just inside the hallway on the floor I saw a claw hammer which I had been using to hang some pictures up the day before. I grab the hammer and start to go after him. My wife grabs my arm, I look up and he's in the van and away.

There was some police involvement but we managed to agree to disagree as to what had actually happened and that was that.

Two lessons have been learned.

1. Always put your boots on, I had a really bad cut on the underside of my right foot.
2. Move the dustbin out of the way.

I had received a phone call from John asking if I wanted to work the weekend. The venue was a pub down in Sunbury where there would be two of us to look after the governor down there.

Pete was having the weekend off and so for the first time my back was going to be watched by a total stranger. Obviously the most important thing in this game is being able to trust the person you're working with. Working with people you don't know can be very costly. You have no idea how they are going to react when situations get ugly.

And believe me if you decide to work on the door you will have plenty of opportunities to get into ugly situations.

I arrive at the venue with more than a little trepidation, as I open the door I am approached by a tall lean fella with a Kiwi accent.

'Hello, mate, I'm Chris.'

My initial level of apprehension was now almost completely gone.

Sometimes you meet someone and almost immediately you know whether or not they are up to the job.

The pub was situated in the middle of a large council estate. It was a traditional old-fashioned looking place complete with a smelly threadbare beer-stained patterned carpet and a light brown nicotine-coated ceiling. The DJ was setting up his 'disco' equipment which consisted of a turntable which sat upon what looked like a modified ironing board flanked on either side by some DIY flashing light units. The landlord was a short arsed mouthy little git and absolutely fitted right in. I don't know who was worse, him or the punters. You would have been hard pressed to find a place with a more concentrated amount of scumbags, it was wall to wall with attitude. You have to use your loaf a bit in places like this; if you give one of these punters a slap you'll probably end up fighting everyone in the pub. What a dump.

Basically the people that frequented the place just wanted to cause us as much grief as possible. Drug-dealing and violence being the staple diet of these folks.

Nice crowd.

We had nothing too serious to deal with though just the usual mindless comments that you have heard a hundred times before.

'What are you fucking bouncers doing in 'ere?'

'You fink you're so fucking 'ard.'

'I'll 'av you, mate. I'll do you up a treat, old son.'

'You're a big bloke but that don't bother me because I know people.'

And my all-time favourite: 'I'll come back and do you, mate, and I've got guns as well.'

THE PEACEMAKERS

A couple of days later the office rang me and asked if Pete and I would come down for a chat; they were going to offer us a more permanent venue.

The venue was in a very affluent part of west London where you can rub shoulders with the rich and famous. Ironically it was a place we had contacted a while back.

A beautiful town during the day, with its large picturesque green where tournaments and pageants were held a few centuries ago, clusters of wonderful little antique shops and cosy little pubs lead you down towards the river where the Kings and Queens of England once made a home for themselves.

After six o'clock, once the shops have battened down the hatches for the night, the place takes on a different kind of feeling. Hordes of youngsters and all kinds of weirdos come out of the woodwork and descend upon it.

It was quite a pleasant looking bar with half a dozen sturdy looking brass lamps hung above the large windows illuminating the name of the place, accompanied by a green sunshade above the front doors. We arrived a little early so we decided to go for a coffee in the nearby restaurant to kill some time. After about fifteen minutes we decided to show our faces. Joyce greeted us at the front doors as we arrived; she was a young fair-haired pretty little Scots woman who had been the manager there for the past three years.

There were four of us on that door, two in-house and two front of house. The two other boys, Dave and Mark, were both very experienced and very confident and definitely could handle themselves. The club had an alarm system with strategically placed alarm buttons, one was just inside the front doors on the floor so a discreet tap with your toe would summon the rest of the boys when things were going pear-shaped. The other one was up by the DJ who incidentally was a right little prima donna. And definitely was more trouble than he was worth. The other thing that annoyed me was that he was on twice as much money as us, it should have been the other way around. Mind you, we used to give him a bit of stick especially if he started to play that RnB music. One of the lads had a quiet word with him one night and he seemed to be as good as gold after that. I never found out what was actually said but he was always very well behaved when this particular person was around. If I were to hazard a guess as to what was said to him it would be something to do with his equipment and a large plate glass window. I do feel that the type of music that was played was important, it sets the tone of the club thereby attracting a certain type of punter and discouraging another. There was some really good dance music around at the time: Robin S, The Nightcrawlers and 'Dreamer' by Livinjoy being my own personal favourite at the time. They all still sound just as good ten years on.

As you entered, on your left was a large L-shaped bar with eight TV screens above it, which showed various endless music videos all night long. To the left of the bar was a small dance floor and a little staircase that lead you up to a raised platform were the DJ was positioned. Straight ahead was a conservatory area with a pool table plus a large beer garden beyond that. At the time it was the most popular pub in the area with the younger generation. Little did I know when I turned up that first night that I would be on that door for the next four years, experiencing some happy and sad occasions, lots of small fights and some that were pretty rough. I had a few laughs as well though.

Pete and I have been here three months now, we've had nothing too serious to contend with so far just a lot of verbal… Mark has now gone, he decided to get involved in some close protection work. Eventually he is replaced by Darren, a big useless lump who lasted about three weeks.

Dave has now moved on which was a shame because we got on well with him; he was a pleasure to work with and was one hundred per cent reliable and trustworthy.

We get a succession of different guys turning up, the first one was Garry, a nice fella but he was a bit too aggressive at times and lacked the diplomacy you need to have in this line of work. The next one to turn up was Alex, a big Scots lad, a nice bloke and a bit of a hard nut, but again aggressive when it wasn't really necessary. I think they just didn't give a toss. An example. One lovely warm summer's evening we were all on the front doors in shirt-sleeve order. The barman comes out to where we were and asks if we could keep an eye on some fella who was acting a little strange and who was also getting a bit abusive. He is pointed out and one of the lads asks him to behave, the right response was not forthcoming and he is asked to leave. He refused, Pete grabs one arm and Alex grabs the other and he is thrown out of the door.

I am outside in my usual position and the guy goes flying past me from a really hard shove off the step, the other two lads go back to their positions just inside the door.

The guy who's been thrown out looks like a right nutter. I was looking for his banjo; he looked like an extra from *Deliverance*. He stands there staring at me from about five or six feet away, teeth clenched with his chin jutting out, his neck stretched to its limit with his eyes bulging looking at me from an obscure angle. That's OK, I don't mind, eyes cannot hurt you and he is outside my exclusion zone. The exclusion zone means that I imagine a circle of about four feet in circumference around me, anyone entering that is in perfect kicking range. He hasn't entered it yet and so doesn't present a problem at the moment. I say to him, on your bike mate, we don't want any trouble now, do we... No reply and no movement. He just kept staring at me with that mental expression on his face. I thought, he'll get fed up with this after a while and disappear. Alex sticks his head out of the doorway and says in a broad Scots accent.

'Are you still here? If you don't fuck off I'll batter you all around the fucking street.'

Here we go, I thought.

This time we did get a reply.

'Fuck off, you Scots git.'

Alex's hairy forearm flashes past my nose, his fist was on a direct collision course with the guy's skull. It sounded like a cricket ball hitting a coconut when it struck.

He goes down flat on his back and almost immediately jumps up again and looks straight at me; he lets out a scream, just like in those war films when the Army are doing their bayonet training: *AAAARRRRGH!*

He comes charging at me. I remained as relaxed as possible until he entered the 'zone'; once that had been breached I released the mother of all front kicks. He ran straight into it thereby doubling the effect of the kick. My right boot connected perfectly with his stomach giving him the full treatment, the force of the kick literally bent him in two.

His feet left the ground and he was airborne and heading backward in the direction he had just come from. Landing about five feet away on his back, for the second time tonight, he was winded, dazed and confused when we got to him; he was then put into two very painful arm locks.

Unluckily for him a copper just happened to be passing and asks our mate on the floor. 'What are you going to do if these nice gentlemen release you?'

The idiot's reply was 'I'm going to fight them.'

He was then given a nice pair of bracelets to wear and was thrown into the back of a waiting police van. The copper came back about an hour later and said that he had to let him go because he started to cry and promised to go home. I had always got on well with the local constabulary… usually.

We were at the front doors one evening in our usual places when a guy comes out from the bar and informs us that some fella, whilst in the middle of a game of pool, has placed a large lock knife on the side of the table. I think that there was a few quid on the game and so he was trying to intimidate the other guy. We go in and whilst one of the other lads talks to the guy to distract him I quickly snatch the knife from the table. He is then thrown out, once outside he asks for the knife back. We told him to fuck off and if he didn't like it he could go to the Old Bill. Unbelievably he did, and about an hour later three stroppy little WPCs turn up demanding that we hand the knife over as we had committed a theft and furthermore if it was not handed over one of us would be arrested. We couldn't believe what we were hearing. What did they want us to do then just let the guy walk out with a fucking great knife in his pocket? They didn't want to listen to anything I had to say they just kept demanding the knife be returned immediately. I didn't have the knife anyway. One of the supervisors from the security company turned up just before the police arrived and so I gave it to him to take back to the office. They didn't believe what I was saying and gave us twenty-four hours to return the knife to the police station, if not they would be back. What a load of old bollocks. The next evening I collected the knife from the office and went to the police station to talk to someone in authority, to see if I could get someone to make sense of the situation. I spoke to the sergeant on duty, his attitude was completely different. He thanked me for taking the knife off the guy and assured me that when the guy turned up to collect it he would be arrested for carrying an offensive weapon. I suppose we got the right result in the end.

Another incident involved three skinheads who decided to throw their weight around. Basically they began to have a go at some Asian fella and his wife. Now this fella was as wide as he was tall and his wife's language would have put Bernard Manning to shame, nice couple. The Asian fella starts to loose his temper, shouting and screaming at the skinheads and they are doing the same back to him, and his wife is giving them a good volley of verbal as well, and I am in the middle. I manage to calm the Asian bloke down a bit and escort him and his wife to the front doors. The skinheads are trying to cause more trouble and start shouting some more abuse; we get the couple outside where the two other lads deal with them. Pete and I go in to find the three skinheads laughing at the thought that they had got the Asian fella thrown out. I go to what seemed to be the ringleader and ask him to put his drink down and leave. He laughs and tells me to fuck off. As soon as he says that my right hand is on his throat and my left hand grabs his right hand, which is still holding a pint glass. There was no point in trying to appeal to their good nature, they had deliberately come here to cause trouble and no amount of good intentioned talking was going to make any difference.

Once you have made the decision to eject someone you have got to go in hard and be totally committed, a half-hearted effort will only give your adversary the opportunity to counter-attack and then *you* will be on the receiving end. If you go in fifty per cent committed you will probably get one hundred per cent battered.

I start to push him backward towards the front doors; halfway there he struggles and digs his heels in and we come to a halt. A knee strike to his stomach gets him going backwards again, I manoeuvre him over to the doors and his mate tries to attack me with a beer glass. Pete grapples with him and then his other mate comes from the other side to attack me. I switch my grip from his throat to a headlock and at the same time I get his mate in the same hold so basically I have both of them in headlocks. I manage to get them outside and throw them out onto the pavement. Pete gets the other one out and the ringleader is thrown to the ground, he sits on the floor and starts to rant and rave about how he is going to come back and sort us out. What he actually said was that he would be coming back to 'Stick a big fucking knife through your head,' pointing at me whilst he said it.

Joyce has a discreet word with me later on and says well done for dealing with those guys. If at any time you want to take someone down into the cellar to give them a good hiding feel free to do so; to look at her you would think butter wouldn't melt… I liked Joyce.

The Asian fella and his wife turn up at around closing time, they are both very drunk and very loud. They start to have a heated argument just outside the entrance to the club. The fella grabs his wife by the lapel and raises his fist. It doesn't look as if this is the first time that they have had this type of altercation, she then smashes a beer bottle on the railings and threatens him with it promising that if he doesn't back off he will be sorry. Joyce was watching what was happening and says that she wants these two barred.

Two weeks on now…

Pete offers to go and get the drinks from next door, and leaves his position up on the little stage area next to the DJ, which was incidentally the best place to scrutinise the crumpet from. I am now alone on the front door. Just as Pete disappears the Asian guy turns up with three of his pals. As he approaches the entrance I say to him that he is barred and will have to drink somewhere else tonight. Which shouldn't have been a problem: there must be at least twenty pubs in the area. Mind you, he's probably barred at most of them.

'Why am I fucking barred then?'

I explain that it was because of the argument he had with his wife a couple of weeks ago.

'I'm going in to see if my wife is in there.'

'You're not going in and she's not in there anyway,' I say to him.

'How do you fucking know that then?'

By now my patience is beginning to wear a little thin. 'Because she's barred as well,' was my reply. With that he started to lose his temper and shaped up as if he wanted to have a go. His friends take hold of him by the arms in an effort to restrain him. I had seen him a while back involved in a brawl and from what I could see as we passed by in the car, he gave a pretty good account of himself.

Having had enough of his insults and threats by now I say to his companions to release him, if he wants to have a go. I knew exactly which technique I was going to use against him.

He wasn't all that tall, probably about five nine. I was standing on the step so the moment he stepped into the exclusion zone the first thing he'd get was a size eleven toe punt right under the chin, basically a front kick to the face. His friends pull him away. At that moment the tea boy arrives.

New Year's Eve: this year seems to have flown by, it never really bothered me working at this particular time of year, we always had a good laugh and there was very little serious trouble to deal with. Most people were just pleasantly pissed and happy and the atmosphere was generally good. Everyone was having a good time, the place was decked out with balloons and streamers; the music was so loud that you could actually see the windows vibrating. We get a shout from one of the barmaids that some fella has passed out on the dance area. I go in to find a big fat bloke lying there with his shirt off, covered in tattoos flat on his back right in the middle of the dance floor. He's a really big lump and must be twenty stone or more. I call for Pete to give me a hand.

We manage to drag him part of the way, not an easy thing to do with the place absolutely heaving. He starts to come around and staggers to his feet, he gets a little aggressive so I give him a good shove towards the door. He stumbles through the door backwards just as Joyce the manager is trying to enter. Joyce is met by his huge arse and is pinned to the wall outside; we come to her rescue and fatty wanders off into the middle of the road where he lays down. They must have thought a new mini roundabout had been built. Joyce thought it was amusing and at the end of the night she bought us all a few drinks. Just as we were leaving, bearing in mind that this is about five hours later, I notice a pair of feet sticking out from behind the fruit machines. It was fatty; he was bedded down for the night.

God knows how he got back in. Joyce beats a hasty retreat behind the bar and fatty is thrown out for the second and last time hopefully.

Happy New Year!

A few months on now…

Just an ordinary Friday evening: Pete and I turn up as usual and assume our positions either side of the front doors. The head barman comes over and asks if he can have a quiet word. I don't like the looks of this, I thought to myself; he goes on to say that he has some sad news… Joyce had died whilst she was on holiday.

She was young, fit and healthy and full of life just a week ago; dead? We couldn't believe it. The place was never quite the same again; it definitely went downhill after that.

The last time I saw her she was happy and singing along to a song with a couple of her friends, so that's how I will remember her.

A succession of managers come and go but then a permanent manager is given the licence. Her name was Jo: a very attractive young woman, slim blonde and in her mid to late twenties, she was also an ex-copper. Fuck me, that's all we need. She would often remind me that she still had her uniform and hand cuffs upstairs, the little devil.

Actually her being ex Old Bill was an advantage for us, she would often have a word on our behalf. When the police turned up to the occasional altercation, she spoke up for me and the lads many times, even when there was more than reasonable force being applied to our attackers. I liked Jo; she was very shrewd but quite shy and vulnerable really, a good-hearted person as well. We had a few laughs with Jo and she would always sort us out with a couple of beers at the end of the night.

A number of different guys are sent down to work with us, some good some bad and some ugly. Paul was one of the new recruits, he was mean looking with his close cropped hair and close shaven beard; he also had a cut running the entire width of his forehead; apparently caused by someone slashing him with a Stanley knife.

I remember one night a very well-known male dancer was walking past; I had seen him walk past quite a few times on his way to the train station which was nearby. I think he was performing at the theatre, which was just around the corner. He had a big bunch of flowers with him. Paul walks over to him and says, 'Have you bought those for me?'

He frightened the life out of him, he did a quick couple of side steps and was away, and I never saw him again. He must have taken the scenic route and bypassed the club from then on. Paul had that effect on some people.

He stayed with us for about six weeks. That was the quietest period I'd ever had at the club, maybe it had something to do with him.

We used to get a few old dossers mooching about, and every Friday night without fail the same one used to turn up and try to get in. He was a small, old Scots guy; he wore a battered old straw trilby hat with tufts of red hair protruding from underneath the brim. He had elastic bands around his shoes to keep the soles on (he was literally on his uppers) and a filthy old jacket and trousers. As he came closer to me I could see the dirt and filth on his shirt, well, it wasn't like dirt, it was probably more like topsoil. It was also a warm night and he was beginning to chuck up big time.

He turns to me and says...

'I'm coming in, who's going to stop me? Hic! Burp! Fart!'

I turned and pointed in the direction of Paul.

'He will.'

'Him…! he should be in a fucking cage.'

He marched up the high street mumbling and shaking his head and I never saw him again.

Paul was asked to take over the door at another venue.

We now have a new member of the team, a tall fair-haired good-looking young fella, with an eye for the ladies. He was called John. We had a slight problem though with John; he was smaller in stature than Pete and myself and so when we had to ask someone to leave they almost always turned around and vented their anger against him. Which was a big mistake because he could handle himself quite well, and coupled with his hot temper it made him quite a handful.

And so there was me, Pete and John; it stayed that way for just over a year.

One of the good things about having John with us was that he had a motor. Pete and I were used to getting the night bus; that bus was murder: everyone was pissed, belching, farting and fighting… the blokes were just as bad.

The other problem you would sometimes encounter was that there was a good chance you would be sitting next to the arsehole you had clumped and thrown out earlier that night.

It was a nice cool spring Saturday evening, Pete had gone next door to get our usual free coffee or tea from the burger bar. The manager used to sort us out with free drinks and towards the end of the evening she would often bring us out something to eat. I helped her out one night when she was having some trouble with a couple of young lads who decided to start to smash the place up. They did employ a security guard; he was a young Indian fella. Some nights we spent as much time in the restaurant helping him as we did in the club. He was a nice guy and so we couldn't just stand by and leave him in the shit. After that we were sorted. John was inside doing an internal patrol, I was on the main entrance.

Pete has arrived back with two coffees and I had my usual cup of strong tea. Pete goes in to give John a shout. He leaves the drinks on the windowsill and goes inside to find him.

After about three or four minutes no sign of either of them. I look into the bar towards the dance floor area, the smoke machine was making it difficult to see clearly but I could just about see Pete moving around. I got the feeling things were not quite right. As I push my way through the crowd I hear the telltale signs of trouble, glasses and bottles being smashed accompanied by muffled shouts and high pitched screams.

At about twenty feet away Pete was being confronted by two young fellas both armed with bottles. He grabs one guy and dislodges the bottle from his hand and throws the fella to the floor. John is exchanging punches with some other fella. He stops fighting and delivers a perfectly timed roundhouse kick to the other guy's face which knocks him out cold, luckily for Pete. The guy was about to bounce a bottle off the back of his skull. John then continues to swap punches with the other fella; just as I get there he draws back his right hand and sends it smashing into the guy's jaw. Everything seems to be in slow motion, that familiar tingling sensation in the pit of your stomach starts to kick in followed by icy cold shots of adrenaline racing through your veins. A pint glass comes flying out of the crowd heading in my direction; it just misses my face and smashes against the wall in front of me sending shards of glass into the air, which are being picked out by the strobe lighting. I didn't see who threw it but sometimes when things kick off other people who are unconnected decide to join in just for fun. John's right-hand punch was now becoming a regular visitor to the guy's face delivering stinging painful blows. This fella was getting a right pasting. He must have received at least half a dozen unanswered punches. I move in on him and put him into the old faithful stranglehold.

As soon as I lock it on he's got no chance, his right hand is searching for a bottle to use against me, he picks up the bottle but with a quick squeeze on his carotid arteries the bottle falls to the floor… he is history.

Dragging him backwards through the crowd I manage to manoeuvre him over to the main entrance. John is right beside me and Pete is now back with us. I turn and face the door and push him outside into the street. Just as I release the hold on him John delivers a perfect right cross which connects on the guy's jaw. The impact sends a thin stream of blood and snot exiting through his mouth and nostrils, which splatters on the wall next to me. Once we were outside I could see the damage that had been inflicted on him.

One side of his face had not been touched while the other side was a real mess and damaged past recognition. A very painful experience, he won't be entering any beauty contests for a while. I went into the Gents to clean the blood from my jacket; when I had put the guy into the stranglehold a fair amount of claret from a bad cut over his eye had leaked out onto my sleeve. I make my way back through the crowd to the front doors to find two police cars and an ambulance on the scene; three of them are taken to the nearest casualty department. The one that Pete had thrown to the floor had landed heavily on his shoulder, one had a bad nosebleed courtesy of John's boot and the other one that John was dealing with was definitely in need of medical attention. John joins them, not in the ambulance but in a police car; he is arrested and is taken to the nearest cell for the night.

Blessed are the peacemakers. Now where's that cup of tea?

The charges were dropped and he was released from custody the next day.

This is a rough game, some people do not respond to reason; the only thing some individuals understand is violence and the threat of violence, it's the only thing they seem to respect. It is a sad absolute fact. That is what happened in this case. The people involved were a very belligerent group of young men; they would not respond to reason instead they decided to use violence against us.

Muppets + drink + drugs = ag.

Some people's Saturday night out solely revolves around going to the clubs and pubs to take on all-comers including the doormen. Why? I don't know. I have never understood that, maybe they have to prove something to themselves. All I know is that we were *prepared* to take on anyone if necessary. And that's the way it was. I don't like violence but you can't talk to some people.

Prepared being the word to consider, I was ready for them. I trained hard and practised as much as I could; that is my edge over my attackers. Without the training you are no better than the person you are dealing with. If you are not prepared, you will probably lose.

The more fights you observe or become involved in the easier fighting becomes. It becomes easier because you can read the signs which gives you the opportunity to anticipate what is going to happen and then react accordingly. You react without thought sometimes, it's like the reaction save of a goalkeeper; he doesn't think about what to do he just does it without thinking. It is what the Japanese refer to as *mushin* which means no mind; like Musashi says, strike from the void. But to get to the stage where you can react correctly without thought takes years of dedicated training, using your whole body as a weapon when delivering your counter-attack. To move and parry your opponent's blow, then return your own devastating crushing blow in one movement. That to me is the essence of karate. If you were to think too much about what you were doing it wouldn't work. When you seek it you cannot find it.

If you fail to prepare be prepared for failure.

It's not all doom and gloom, we had some good laughs as well. I used to go to the office at Ealing to collect the wages for the lads on Saturday evenings so I was sometimes a little late arriving at the club.

This particular Saturday had just seen the defeat of the South African rugby team at Twickenham. The club was full of rugby supporters who had decided to bring in off the street the dirtiest old tramp they could find; they sat him in the middle of the dance area where he was given a steady supply of ale.

His hair was grey and matted, one side sticking up and the other side as flat as a pancake; he was wearing a vest which had taken on a life all of it's own covered in some very dodgy looking stains. He was only a little fella but the jacket he had on was easily four sizes too big and the trousers were straight out of Charlie Chaplin's wardrobe which were pulled right up to his chest, basically when he moved the suit followed a moment later. He's got to go; I put my gloves on and get one of the other doormen to come with me to escort the old fella outside. Going through the crowd he started to respond to the shouts and jeers from the rugby supporters who found the whole scenario very amusing. He was starting to struggle and as we were passing a couple of attractive young women who were seated by the door, he decided to dig his heels in. A scuffle began, the timing could not have been better; as if on cue his trousers dropped to his ankles and minus any underwear therefore treating the two young women to a full frontal. A loud cheer went up and the whole place erupted into laughter.

Eventually we manage to throw him out. We watched him as he zigzagged up the high street still holding a bottle of beer, with trousers at half mast singing away without a care in the world. Brilliant, what a way to start the evening.

Another humorous situation occurred with the return of a peculiar woman who we had barred a couple of weeks earlier. She was basically very drunk and abusive, and was asked to leave the premises. It was not my fault that as she went through the door she tripped and fell on her arse. She had thought I had tripped her up; blaming everyone for her embarrassing predicament she then picks herself up and continues her tirade of foul language in our direction. She fell over because she was blind drunk. Perhaps I am a bit old-fashioned but to see a young woman in this state makes a very depressing spectacle. Initially you find it mildly amusing but when you think about it, it's a bit sad really. Unfortunately it is a common occurrence in this game and dealing with them is all part of the job.

It was getting near to last orders and we still had a small queue at the front doors when this old trout turns up and walks straight to the front much to the annoyance of a big fella who was next in line. She was ranting and raving and demanding to be allowed in. I was called to deal with the situation. I told her she had no chance and basically to go away or words to that effect. (It was the same woman who I had barred the previous Saturday.)

With that the big fella butted in, 'Can I go in now, mate?'

Before I could say a word she screams at him and tells him to fuck off at the top of her voice and then she takes a huge swing at him. He manages to avoid her punch and then the bell for last orders is rung. A red mist must have descended over this normally peaceful individual; he was not worried about being attacked by this mad woman, but because of her the frightening prospect of not getting in to savour the last few pints of his Saturday night out was becoming a reality.

It's all too much for him and a peach of a right-hand punch catches her flush on the chin; Mike Tyson would have been proud of that one. She goes down and gets up to stagger down the road holding her chin, not too much to say now, I thought.

I told fatty off for what he done; he was very apologetic, and then I let him in so he could purchase his well-deserved pint. To the victor the spoils.

Don't get me wrong, I am not condoning violence against a woman but this person would not respond to normal requests, she was ruining everyone's night out, threatening us all at the door, she used so many expletives she actually ran out of them and then tried to use violence because she could not get her own way, just the sort of girl you could bring home to meet your mother.

She was drunk, violent and foul and got what she deserved. The fairer sex... my arse.

Peter, John and myself were standing outside the front doors one warm summer evening, the usual crowds are all filing past when I notice a young woman walk past.

She stops suddenly, turns around and comes back in our direction and enters the bar. About thirty seconds later we hear screams and that telltale sound of breaking glass, the alarm is sounded and we rush in to find that the young girl who had just walked in had smashed a pint glass over some guy's head.

Pete is the first one inside and he grabs the young woman, she is going ballistic, shouting and screaming at some fella who was sitting by the window. Pete puts her in the stranglehold, after all this is the nineties, equality and all that. And so she is thrown out just like any other violent person. Male or female they are all treated the same. As she goes past me I notice that she has a cut to her right hand, she then sprints up the road and disappears. Actually we should have kept her there in case the guy wanted to press charges. I'm glad we didn't in the end because he was a right little wanker.

John is busy throwing the guy out of the door who has a nasty looking couple of cuts to his scalp and blood trickling down his forehead; he has also got some small shards of glass sticking out of the top of his head.

The guy wasn't too happy about being thrown out and starts to try and go back into the bar. John grabs him by the collar from behind and yanks him off the step and back outside; he must have pulled the guy really hard because as he done so the whole back of the guy's shirt comes away in John's hands. It was like something out of a Laurel and Hardy film. He turns around in disbelief and points at John and says:

'You owe me a fucking new shirt, you bastard!'

We don't generally respond too well to that kind of behaviour. John walks over to him calls him a stupid prick and laughs in his face. He's standing outside with pieces of glass in his head, blood trickling down his face, wearing half a shirt, also the girl he had been with in the bar has done a runner. I would imagine he has had better nights out.

What happened was that this fella had been seen through the window with another young woman, his regular girlfriend spotted him as she walked past. She enters the club and smashes a pint pot over his head, he then takes a swing at her and the rest you know.

Young love, all together now, ahhhhhhh.

Pete and I turn up as usual but John is replaced by the guy who was the regular doorman at that horrible little place down in Sunbury. I thought it was a bit odd, as the office would normally tell me if there were to be any changes.

So we have got this fella and John has gone down to the pub in Sunbury with Alex and Garry, the two doormen that have been mentioned earlier.

We've only been there about half an hour when the alarm goes off; as soon as that alarm goes off you get an instant massive hit of adrenaline surging through you. Pete and I go in to find two groups of young fellas, about eight or nine of them, are involved in a mass brawl. Two guys are rolling around on the floor, punching, nutting and kicking each other, the rest of them were all engaged in one big scrap where boots and fists are all being used in a high speed frantic tangle of bodies. Chris, the other doorman, has got two of the guys in headlocks and is pulling them towards to exit. We quickly get to grips with the situation where Pete and I administer strangleholds all round. We separate them and start to eject the ringleaders. I was surprised that there weren't any serious injuries to deal with. All of the troublemakers have been dealt with and things are back to normal, when I notice that my boots have a splattering of blood on them; we then notice a trail of blood leading from the front doors along the pavement and up the high street.

At the top of the road were a couple of the lads we had thrown out, one of them was sitting on the pavement holding the side of his head. As I got a bit closer I could see blood running between his fingers and down the side of his face and neck. I asked him if I could see the injury and as he took his hand away I could see that he had been given a 'Van Gogh': his ear had almost been sliced in two.

He had been slashed with a very sharp knife. An ambulance was called and the wounded soldier was carted off and stitched up and would live to fight another day. But not in our club. He was lucky; an inch or two lower and it would have severed an artery. What a nasty little violent world we live in.

I was thinking, I bet John is having a nice quiet evening chatting up all the women. Actually nothing could have been further from the truth. The two lads who were working with him had some problems with a pikey earlier on. They had been given the usual verbal threat of him coming back to sort them out later on with a few of his pals.

Most of the time nothing happens; it is just someone trying to salvage a bit of pride, but you have always got to be ready for the possibility that they will carry out the threat. You have to stay switched on and you're not to let complacency set in.

Every doorman's nightmare suddenly became a brutal reality; the guy did come back and with his pals; also they all had decided to bring a claw hammer each. They then proceeded to take the place apart. They smashed everything in the pub including Garry and Alex. They were beaten to the floor and given the full treatment with hammer and boot. The two lads had a variety of injuries as you can imagine and were hospitalised for a while; they are tough lads and recovered with no lasting problems. John had survived the affair with little or no injuries, he was lucky. There was something of the inevitable about that, it was just waiting to go off in that place.

John was back with us the next week but didn't seem to

be his old self. I think he was still suffering from what had happened the week before.

It was getting near to closing time, last orders had been called and the two lads adopted their usual positions either side of the main doors, which was now a one-way door, out only. I go in to get the punters moving when I notice that Jo, the manager, seemed to be having a few problems with a couple of guys. I make my way over behind them and overhear Jo tell them that she wants them to leave; one of the lads says, I'm not being thrown out by a barmaid.

'Barmaid? I'm the manager I don't have to throw you out anyway; I have security they do that for me,' Jo says.

No poxy doorman's going to throw me out was the reply. I step forward and take over the conversation; I could see where this one was going.

'Put your drinks down, lads, you are being asked to leave.'

Fuck off was his response; he had now also adopted a more aggressive attitude.

My kind and courteous manner was being perceived as a weakness and I was rewarded with abuse; violence being imminent I take the initiative.

I grab his throat with one hand and take hold of his other hand, which contains a pint glass. John has made his way over and Pete stays in position on the front door.

I push him over to the front doors where Pete puts him into a stranglehold, he was struggling away but once that hold is locked on you're finished. As I turn around I was confronted by a mate of his, what we had not realised was that there were seven of them; aggrieved at the fact their friend had been ejected, they all decided to converge on yours truly.

The first attacker came forward in a boxing type pose

and started to swing wildly with lefts and rights aiming them at my head. I threw a hard fast right cross, it was just a natural reaction, a strike from the void perhaps. It connected smack on the guy's chin; he did a 360 and spiralled down to the floor and out. I kept moving around with my hands in the ready position; everywhere I looked someone was coming at me. The next combatant threw a punch at John, which missed. John was more accurate with his and a hard left hand smacks into the guy's jaw, which sent him stumbling in my direction. A right-hander from me sends him over to Pete and he is dumped outside on the pavement. The next one again adopts some form of fighting stance; he was a little bigger than the others. He came forward with his fists clenched and decided to try his luck. Before he had time to think about what he was going to do I move slightly to my right and deliver a quick, accurate, powerful open-hand strike. It was a technique that I had practised for years; it went through his guard and the palm of my right hand struck him in the centre of the chest. The impact sent him flying backwards and he went upside down over a table full of drinks, sending glasses, bottles and punters in all directions. Now we had two outside and two on the deck, three to go. When they saw their mate go flying over the table it must have sent the right message; they decided to fight another day. They tiptoed over their fallen comrades and walked out under their own steam. I would imagine the whole thing was over in less than thirty seconds but when it's actually happening it seems a hell of a lot longer than that. I took no chances; you can't, especially nowadays, anyone that presented themselves as a target was treated as one. Remember the Queensbury rules go out the window and we are going home in one piece and that's all that really mattered.

It was time to lock up; the rest of the evening's revellers were very accommodating at chucking out time; it only took about ten minutes to clear the place.

Jo asks if we would like to stay for a few beers and so after a great deal of arm-twisting we were treated to a few well-deserved pints.

John would almost always have a young lady waiting for him and tonight being no exception, his chat up lines seemed to have paid off and one was waiting outside. We finished our drinks, said good night to Jo and jumped into John's motor, which was a bit of a struggle at the best of times; the car was only a Mini Metro. I let Pete get in first and John's date jumps in the back with him, talk about thick: if her brains were made of dynamite she wouldn't have had enough to blow her hat off. Mind you I don't think he was too interested in what she had between her ears.

John drops Pete and me off back at my place. Wife and kids were in bed hours ago, the fridge was stocked before I left that evening so we chill out with an ice-cold beer and listen to a bit of Pink Floyd whilst mulling over the night's shenanigans.

St Patrick's day: all was going well until... we spot someone in the bar who had decided to take his boots and socks off and place them on the bar, he was about six feet tall with long frizzy red hair and of a robust type of build. He was with about seven or eight of his pals and they were all knocking back copious amounts of the black stuff and getting very loud and boisterous. He was asked to put his boots back on but refused at first. Here we go again, I thought. I told him to stop acting like a 'gob shite'. I figured he might understand if I asked him using some of his own terminology, and after that he reluctantly did as I asked. We are all back at the front door when eight or nine other Irish fellas try to enter the club. They have all had way too much to drink and so we knock them back, they are not too pleased with being refused entry and decided to give us a lot of verbal and start to crowd the door. Meanwhile the fella who had his boots off earlier is trying to tell us that the guys outside are his mates and they will behave themselves, and he starts to tell them to come in. Here we go: nine outside eight inside and we are in the middle outnumbered as usual. You get this lot together and there will be murders. So I push him back into the bar and put my foot against the inner door to prevent him and his mates getting at us from behind. Just as I am doing that one of them jumps up and throws a punch over his mate's shoulder, which smacks John right in the eye. As soon as the blow lands, the three of us burst forwards out of the doorway to engage them in a mass brawl. At that moment a police van screeches to a halt right outside the club.

Lucky for them, we were up for that one and I guarantee you that a few of them would have never forgotten that particular St Patrick's day. One of the coppers comes over and takes a look at John's eye (which is rapidly turning into a nice little shiner), he asks if he wants to press charges to which John replied no but I want to take him around the corner for a straightener. The chap who had thrown the punch overhears the remark and a scuffle ensues between John, this bloke and two coppers; two other paddys started to give the Old Bill some verbal and refused to move and so with a bit of a struggle they were arrested. We managed to get rid of them, the ones who were inside as well. About twenty minutes later three of them came back and apologised for their friend's behaviour because apparently it had nothing to do with them. The older guy who is about fifty odd says to me that he is a gentleman and doesn't want any trouble and promises to behave; 'Bollocks, you've got no chance,' was my reply. He went mental, and started shouting and screaming, his actual words were: 'I'm going to rip your fecking head off.' Stupid old git; he wouldn't have been able to punch a dent in a pound of butter. His two companions try to restrain him but he was having none of it; my patience now exhausted I decide to give him an opportunity to carry out his threat. I step out of the door and challenge all three to have a go; they declined my offer and beat a hasty retreat back to the Emerald Isle. To be sure, to be sure.

We stay for a while after closing up and have our usual couple of drinks with Jo, but on this particular occasion we are joined by one of the new barmaids. She's a big old sort, about five foot two and she's got to be weighing in at around the sixteen stone mark, she therefore acquired the unflattering title of 'the big 'un'; she's a bit fruity as well (a dangerous combination). She was wearing a tight-fitting short skirt and a blouse that must have been a couple of sizes too small; the buttons on it were under an enormous amount of strain trying desperately to contain her huge knockers and rolls of fat. Pete said that she had touched him up earlier on that night (fuck me, she must be desperate). She sat down and joined in the conversation and announces that she has been taking classes in the art of massage. I just happen to mention to her that John had been complaining of a bad back earlier in the evening (he hadn't been). She then decided to give a practical demonstration. John's shirt disappeared in a flash, suddenly finding himself half-naked and at the mercy of a sex-starved sumo in knickers. He was put into a half nelson and placed face down over a table where she now went to work on him, her chubby digits prodding and poking him all over. She looked over at me and says: 'You're next, big boy.'

I decided that a tactical withdrawal might be a good idea. I was out that door like a fucking rocket.

John decided to part company with us and set up his own business, best of luck to him. I'm going to miss working with him. He backed us up without fail every time when things kicked off, he would get right in the thick of things trading blows with the best of them. The three of us made a pretty good team. He was a bit of a tearaway though.

We now have a replacement for him; he was about twenty, a bit too young for this game really, but we will try and look after him. Mind you he didn't look as if he needed looking after, he was built like a brick shit house. He had a shaven head with tattoos all over the place. After a few weeks we all got on really well, he was a likeable guy but had a violent temper. Which I think unfortunately is going to get him into serious trouble one day.

His name was Simon. I tried to show him the finer points of door etiquette, diplomatic ways in which you could escort a difficult punter off the premises without too much effort. His way was to engage the transgressor in a very short verbal exchange combined with a head butt between the eyes.

What we have here is a failure to communicate.

The office rang me and asked if Pete and I would look after a club down in Greenford. We got to the office and had a quick chat with John, he asked one of the supervisors to run us down there. Halfway through the journey the supervisor says he is glad he hadn't been asked to look after this place tonight; he thought it was a bit dodgy. Why? Where are you going? I say.

'I'm going to look after a pub in the East End later on tonight.'

Apparently it was a popular underworld haunt. He doesn't fancy a night in Greenford but has no problem working in the East End for some well-known gangsters. Does he know something we don't? I asked him what the SP was down here, he says that the doormen who used to work there were not best pleased in losing their venue and that there was talk of reprisals against anyone who took over the door; guess what, this was the first night.

Fuck them; if they try anything they'll come unstuck. We're not stupid, we have back up that we can call upon if necessary.

We eventually arrive at the place; the supervisor didn't hang about, waving to us as he shot out of the car park with wheels spinning and disappears in a cloud of dust.

It was a big venue with a largely Irish clientele. Two huge front doors lead you into a porch area, which is where we positioned ourselves for the evening.

We had a CCTV monitor just inside the door; it had a quartered split screen giving us an all-round view of the place. Inside was a long straight bar with six or seven very busy staff rushing about behind it.

A large stage to the rear and in front of that about a hundred chairs had been set out.

As the live band was setting up the manager came out to give us the once over. I asked one of the barmen what the previous door staff were like, he said that they were three very arrogant young Asian lads; one in particular would occasionally demonstrate his dexterity with a butterfly knife spinning it around in his hand in full view of the punters. The barman was asked by the manager to stay with us and point out any undesirables, he also had to stay there and collect the £5 entrance fee.

The place was starting to fill quite rapidly, they all seemed in good spirits, everyone seemed to be acting perfectly normal. As the band starts to play their first number some fella gets up on to the stage and starts crawling about, we both go in and to the cheers of the crowd pick the guy up by his arms and deposit him back into his seat.

It was all very light-hearted and the band started to play on. Two minutes later he's up again, this time trying to give his own rendition of 'My Way'. He's got to go this time. We drag him off the stage to loud applause and dump him outside on the pavement.

He starts to argue a bit and the manager comes over to intervene. He says to the guy he can come back in if he agrees to behave himself. I suggested that he let us deal with him, clearly he has had way too much to drink and is only going to get worse. But the manager says he will give him one last chance to behave and so he goes back in and almost immediately is up on the stage giving an Elvis impression. It was quite amusing but he is going out for good this time. We drag him off the stage and throw him outside. I stay just inside the door and Pete is on the outside, I ask Pete to keep an eye on him as he walks up the road.

'What's that bloke doing now, mate?'

'He's getting into a rubbish skip.'

'You what?'

'What's he doing now?'

'He's getting out of the skip and he's got a big lump of wood.'

'What's he doing now?'

'He's swinging it around his head and he's coming back towards the pub.'

I didn't see the barman leg it, I just felt the wind as he went past disappearing into the back of the beer garden some fifty yards away.

As he gets closer to the venue I go out to face him while Pete goes to one side. He looks at me and then at Pete, we are both either side of him; we get a closer look at the lump of wood he had taken out of the skip: it was a four-foot piece of three by two with two or three large crooked nails sticking out of one end.

Nasty little bastard, I thought. He had it in a two-handed baseball bat type grip. Before he had time to think about who he was going to whack first, I move forward which distracted him for a second. Pete then quickly moved in from the side and snatched the weapon out of his hands. The longer the delay in this type of scenario the worse it becomes; they will begin to gain in confidence, move in hard and fast. Ordinarily in this type of dangerous confrontation once we had disarmed him he would have got a right pasting but he was so pathetic. All he got was a hard slap across the chops and boot up the arse from Pete.

We also let him know that if he came anywhere near the place tonight that he would most definitely be feeling the worse for wear in the morning. I looked at my watch; we had only been at the place an hour.

There were no more incidents that night, in fact it turned out to be one of the best nights that we had ever done; a steady supply of drinks (soft drinks) were supplied by the bar staff. We never had more than two halves of lager each whilst we were working on the door. After, yes, during, no, that was part of our unwritten code. The band dedicated their last number to the two lads on the door: it was called 'Black Velvet'; the very attractive lead singer did an excellent rendition. She was looking at me all through the song, well, that's what I told Pete anyway. We were paid some very fine compliments that night by staff and punters who had thought we had done a very professional job.

All that stuff about the previous doormen coming back to sort us out, that was just the usual load of old bollocks. All talk.

The next venue we were going to look after was a large place in Ealing, a very busy bar just by the green; there was four or sometimes five of us on that door, we had worked here before a couple of times so we knew the routine.

Pete and I worked inside and let the regular team sort out the front. They knew all the faces that weren't welcome, not much point us being on the front doors, we may be letting in punters who had been barred. There was one large staircase where one of us would stand and the other one would be positioned above at some distance away on a high balcony which overlooked the whole of the ground floor area. Communication was the problem in this place; the music being deafening put the block on using the radios so we acquired a small flashlight each and worked out a couple of signals. Two flashes for assistance, keeping it simple is the name of the game. I was standing on the large staircase, my feet being at about head height of the customers sitting below me. I suddenly felt a hand slowly creeping up the inside of my trouser leg. I was a bit worried about looking down, I just hope that's a woman's hand I was thinking to myself, there are some very weird people about, you know. I looked down and was relieved to see a very pretty young woman attached to the other end. She was a regular from the other club just having a bit of a laugh with her mates. We only had one idiot to deal with: this guy had decided that he didn't want to leave at closing time and that he was going to finish the two pints he had left and there was no way he was leaving before he had done so. We have the place cleared apart from the arsehole who by now is just starting on his second pint; he has disregarded the polite manner in which he was being asked to leave. I have had enough of this; we will be here all night with this bloke. I ask him to put his drink down and leave the premises.

'Fuck off, I'm finishing my drink.'

An attitude adjustment is required. My own particular way to adjust this type of punter's attitude went something like this. As soon as he said that, as far as I'm concerned he leaves me with very little choice, a left-handed slap down and grab onto his right wrist with an immediate right-handed grip onto the throat, now I have control. You have to do it really quick and with power, otherwise you'll lose the initial momentum; he's a big lad about six two and roughly fifteen stones but once you have the momentum going it's not too difficult to get them where you want them to go. Pushing him backward towards the exit with Pete going in front to open the doors, we manage with a bit of a struggle to throw him outside. We pass the manager who was looking a little concerned at what was happening; as we close the doors the manager says: 'That was a bit rough.'

It wasn't. In fact it was a very controlled exhibition of a perfectly executed ejection technique. Look, at the end of the day the guy was drunk and started to get a little aggressive. Who knows that last pint he wanted to finish may have just been enough to tip him over the edge and become violent. I dealt with him before he got to that stage; he was thrown out suffering an injury only to his pride. I turned to the manager and suggested to him that he didn't have a clue what he was talking about and furthermore I would not try to tell him how to pour a pint of beer. My guess is that the manager was probably fairly new to this game and has rarely seen a punter being treated in this manner.

As we were leaving the place the guy who had been thrown out had decided to wait outside with a friend and engaged us with a few choice words; well, I think we have heard all that before and decide to ignore it. They were just a pair of pissed up pricks looking for trouble, who got their courage from the bottom of a beer glass.

As we started to walk away Pete notices that they are starting to follow us.

'OK, Pete, we'll go this way across the green and into the dark. If they want to have a go I'll choose when and where.'

We take a slight detour and lead them unsuspectingly into the middle of the green.

They continue to follow shouting abuse all the way. We slow down a bit because we are roughly in the middle of the green and in a nice little area, in the dark with no one else around, just where I want them. We allow them to get close enough and then decide to turn and confront our pursuers. They were surprised to see us turn around and face them, turning the tables as it were. The hunters now becoming the hunted, it suddenly dawned on them that they might have been lured into a trap. They had thought our bottle had gone and that we weren't going to do anything. I turn and give the guy who had all the mouth a hard shove into the chest; Pete challenges the other guy who runs away leaving his mate alone in the dark and in the shit.

The shove was intended to do two things, the first was to get him to launch his attack thereby suckering him into a powerful back kick to the stomach, which he definitely deserved after the amount of abuse and threats he was dishing out. The push away also gives you the right distance to execute the technique which I had practised hundreds of times in the little gym, an extremely effective strike and a definite finisher when done correctly. Fortunately for him I didn't have to use it, his bottle went completely and he also decided to run away shouting as he ran that if we touched him he would go to the police. Just like a lot of these types of 'weekend warriors' when it came down to it all he could do was talk like a hard man. You have to be ready though; encounters with these types of characters can be very unpredictable. Sometimes your challenge will be accepted, remember never underestimate anyone. I have a feeling that I might run into these fellas again one day.

Pete and I were back at our usual venue the next week, we had decided that we were only going to work here from now on, our particular way of working not being appreciated elsewhere. Jo was very pleased if not relieved to see our return. She told me that there had been some trouble during the past couple of weeks and was more than a bit concerned with what was happening. Probably down to Simon with his own unique brand of door supervising. *Nut first and ask questions later.*

I must admit there are a few undesirable characters in and definitely some that I have barred in the past, time for a bit of scumbag cleansing. One guy was a dealer that I had barred two years ago, he must have been waiting for me to have a night off so he could ply his trade again. He was a strange character. Black and of medium build, he looked like he was trapped in a 70s time warp complete with flares and a large brimmed hat plus shades of course. I remember a couple of years back he would try all kinds of variations of what he was wearing to gain access.

He was very compliant and left immediately he knew we

were not going to fuck around with him. I have no time for drug dealers; they are near the lowest of the low, the absolute dregs of society as far as I'm concerned.

Jo comes out to the front doors where Pete and I are and informs us that a known dealer is on the premises. She tells us that someone from the drugs squad wanted to have a word with him, she gets a call from the drugs squad saying that they are very busy and will pick him up another time but meanwhile they want us to leave him alone and we are not to touch him, yeah right. Pete and I look at each other and without a word we make our way over to our friendly neighbourhood drug dealer: he was a small thin black guy with shoulder length dreadlocks, which contained a variety of small, coloured beads. He wasn't alone, he had three associates with him: two large black fellas who were both about the same size as me and a young white guy who thought he was the daddy.

We manage to separate the dealer from his companions and take him into the Gents where we tell him that he is leaving; he was more than a little nervous now that he had been separated from his minders. He was visibly shaking as Pete put his boot to the bottom of the door to stop anyone coming in; we did put the frighteners on him a bit though, he thought we were going to give him a kicking; I don't know why! It was probably the way I was holding him by the throat that gave him the idea. But we didn't, all we wanted to do was to get them out of our club. I pushed him over to the urinal trough and told him that we didn't want scumbags like him on the premises and he is to leave immediately. And he is not to go over to his companions but just to go straight to the main exit.

He agreed. On leaving the Gents he quickly makes his way over to his mates. I was right behind him, I thought he might seek the sanctuary of his friends, after all how can you trust the word of a drug dealer? He doesn't quite make it. Intercepted by me I grab him around the neck from behind with one arm and with the other I grab his dreadlocks and drag him backwards through the crowd and throw him out and down onto the pavement. His mates are following right behind trying to rescue him; Pete is pushing and shoving them out of the main exit. All of them have been ejected and are now giving it big style; they were all making that stupid sucking of the teeth noise and gesturing with their hands mimicking the using of pistols. Threats of reprisals are coming thick and fast mainly from the younger white lad; apparently he's going to go home and come back to shoot us all later on. After about five minutes I had started to lose it, I'd had enough of the bullshit. With fists clenched I step outside and confront them, shit or bust, let's have some, I thought, now they have the opportunity to carry out their threats. I walk right up to them and shout:

'Come on then, let's fucking do it!'

I wanted one of them to make a forward move but just like a lot of these types of incidents when it came down to it none of them decided to accept my offer, they were all mouth and no bottle. They all backed down and walked away.

I shouldn't have gone outside of the club, our job was done, they were out so no need to get involved any further. I think the job was definitely getting to me, my tolerance barriers were becoming far too easy to breach. I must admit I wanted to take them on, at that moment when I walked out of the door of the club I wasn't aware of anything; the other lads as far as I was concerned didn't exist. I just had one thought, steam straight in and smash them to bits.

On leaving the club that night just as we were about to

get into the motor we hear someone shouting in our direction. I thought it was the drug dealer and his mates coming back for a tear up but no, it was someone else shouting some form of abuse at Pete.

He thought it might have been someone he had barred a while back; this guy was a young stocky black lad of no more than about twenty, twenty-two max. Basically he was showing off in front of a large group of his pals shouting at the top of his voice. I tell him to shut the fuck up, he tells me to come and shut him up, such arrogance can only be rewarded in one way, his challenge was accepted. Pete could see what was going to happen and says: 'Ignore it, let's get in the motor.'

Which was probably sound advice. It was not long after the encounter with the drug dealer so my blood was still up. I could hear more abuse coupled with laughter. I wasn't having it, who does he think he is? Within a few seconds I was halfway across the road ready to do battle with our tormentor. As I approached he started to dance about giving a pathetic Bruce Lee impersonation, he thought it was all a big joke. I didn't say anything; I just moved in quickly, closed the gap and clumped him really hard. A powerful right hook smashed into the side of his skull, just as I threw the punch he lent forward a fraction in an effort to duck out of the way and so the blow didn't find its correct target area. It was a very powerful blow, which actually upended him; one minute his head was there the next thing I saw was his feet. Who's laughing now? The blow had broken one of the knuckles in my right hand, which was starting to swell up big time; it didn't matter though, I still had my left.

The guy was on his back as Simon came running over and he decided to give his own rendition of River Dance on the guy's head stamping repeatedly on his nose. I stopped him after two or three stamps; he was looking as if he was enjoying it a bit too much. Then one of his pals decides to help his fallen comrade, Simon deals with him by literally kicking his arse up and down the high street. The busy traffic had come to a halt to view the spectacle, a double-decker bus pulls up and the driver decides to stick his head out of the window to have a go at us. I tell him to mind his own business; the way we were carrying on he was lucky he didn't get a slap as well. He got the message and fucked off sharpish. Must be a full moon out tonight or something.

Pete had decided to call it a day. He said that he'd had enough basically. He had been showing signs of disinterest for a while, he wasn't training as much as he used to either so it came as no surprise really. He suggested that we both turn it in. We had started together so we probably should have finished at the same time.

I decided to stay on. What can I say about Pete, his friendship and loyalty were greatly appreciated. It takes a considerable amount of courage to do this job, especially the way we did it. I knew that without a doubt he would be there when I needed him and vice versa. We always got on well; I don't think we ever had a disagreement in all the years I've known him. He could be very witty at times as well, which always helped during the more stressful moments.

The scars you acquire while exercising courage will never make you feel inferior.

D A Battista

MY MANOR

We have a new member of the team to replace Pete. He was a mate of Simon's; small in stature but relatively confident and likeable. He was in his mid to late twenties and seemed to be able to act as a calming influence over Simon, which is not a bad thing.

A week after Pete had left the two guys with whom we had a run in at Ealing turned up in the queue. They were a little bit taken aback to see me and a bit apprehensive to say the least; they both apologised and promised to behave themselves. I let them in, but inside I knew that it would not be long before these two caused some sort of trouble thereby giving us the opportunity to give them a couple of slaps. We didn't have to wait long; the two boys started on a couple of younger lads who were just having a quiet night out with their girlfriends. They were both small guys, one of them was really skinny, I'd seen more fat on Frankie Dettori's whip. The two couples leave the club closely followed by our two brave hard men, outside the club the fight begins with the two smaller guys taking a hammering. One of them is being repeatedly punched and kicked all over the place, the fight has moved away from the club and is now continuing in front of a lovely little Mexican restaurant which was about thirty feet away. Tables, chairs and plants are all being knocked about as the mindless assault continues. The two young women are hysterically shouting and screaming in our direction gesturing for our assistance. One of the lads goes down on his back; the two attackers now take it in turn to stamp and kick the poor guy in the head. Taking two full-blooded boots to the skull, which put the guy out cold and now helpless. We could hear the sound of the boots going in from where we were standing; two more sickening powerful kicks are slammed into the side of his lifeless head. Simon and his mate are like a couple of pitbulls straining at the leash in anger at what they are watching. They turn to me and ask if we should get stuck into them; usually we don't involve ourselves in what is going on outside; we are here to look after the club and the people inside it, but there are exceptions to the rule. I unleash the two lads and they set about mauling one of the attackers to the ground where all sorts of dirty tricks are being used as Simon initiates the rescue by smashing his forehead into the guy's nose. I grab the other one and give him two powerful knee strikes into the stomach; he doubles over where he gets a right hook to the jaw, which was enough to end the assault. The guy didn't want to know, repeatedly saying, 'I don't want to fight you, mate.' As he goes down to the pavement he curls himself up into a ball so I couldn't get a clean shot at him. Not so brave now, I thought.

I call the two lads back in. Simon and his mate had done the other bloke up like a kipper, his eye and nose were pouring with claret from the expert use of Simon's forehead. I don't know what would have happened if we had not moved in to put an end to the attack, how many kicks to the head does it take before a fatality occurs?

The next night we had a little more trouble with a couple of guys who wouldn't do as they were asked, three times I had asked them if they wouldn't mind taking their feet off the seats. Every time my back was turned they put them back up again, fourth time now and I've had enough.

These boys are most definitely looking for trouble.

'OK fellas, you two are leaving.'

He still had his feet up on one of the little cast-iron stools. We are not going anywhere, he says. I pull the stool out from under his feet and he jumps up and adopts a fighting pose, his friend does likewise. He beckons me forward saying, 'Come on. Come on.'

I deliver a hard front kick to his knackers; he stopped talking and fell on the floor clutching his privates. Then to my surprise Simon bursts through the door and takes the other guy out and down to the floor with a very graceful dive and at the same time putting the guy into some mysterious form of a head lock; he's got to stop watching that American wrestling. We get them outside and they decided to make a stand. The smaller of the two makes a lunge at Simon and is put to the ground where he receives half a dozen blows from Simon's sovereign encrusted fist into his face. His companion decides to take off his belt which had a very heavy looking oval-shaped brass buckle attached to it and proceeds to advance swinging his belt around his head in my direction. I stayed just inside the doorway where his weapon of choice would have little effect. All the time that this is happening I was getting the usual threats of violence. What they actually said repeatedly was that this was their manor and they would be back tomorrow to settle the matter. These types of encounters will expose your every weakness if you allow them to. You have to fight against all negative thoughts, stand your ground and '*show no fear*'.

The threats were all said in a very calm and deliberate fashion and my life was threatened in no uncertain circumstances. It's a funny feeling someone telling you that they are going to kill you but you sort of get used to it. I said: 'I'll be here, see you tomorrow then.'

Their parting shot was to throw one of the heavy signboards in our direction, which was ironically advertising the happy hour. It crashed into the door, and cracked the window. Jo was not too happy; I couldn't say that I was either. In actual fact the more I thought about these two the more enraged I was becoming. That was the lowest I have ever felt whilst working at the club.

If I had a pound for every time someone had threatened to shoot me I'd be a very rich man. Why should I think this time would be any different from all the others? I don't know perhaps I'm becoming paranoid or maybe it's because John and Pete aren't around. I will be here tomorrow so we'll see what happens. They were a couple of nasty characters, their threats were taken seriously and so I may have to introduce them to a couple of friends of mine. The bruising irons, as they were affectionately known.

After you have worked in a certain place for a while, especially in this type of occupation, you seem to acquire a certain amount of territorial pride as I call it. Wrong perhaps to think in these terms but nevertheless you do tend to think this way after a while and so that's one reason why some people may stand their ground in these situations. But I think it could simply come down to what kind of person you are inside. Some people refuse to be intimidated and decide to fight back.

It had been raining for most of the day and was steadily getting worse by the evening; it was cold, damp and miserable. I drove through the wet streets at a slow sedate pace thinking of what the night could possibly bring. I wouldn't say that I was feeling scared, if I were I would have stayed at home. I think my mind was quite clear and calm but I was definitely feeling apprehensive about the situation. After all what if these two actually turn up; I will have to live with the consequences of my actions if it all goes pear-shaped. Are they a couple of bullshitters or are they up for it? At the end of the day they are the ones who have threatened me and so whatever happens to them will be of their own making.

I parked the car in the multi-storey car park, which was a few minutes' walk away from the club. I knew the guy in the security box at the car park so he used to let me park there for free which was handy because there's absolutely nowhere to park in this area. I never parked in the same place twice, I would also vary my times as well. You've got to stay one jump ahead of your potential ambushers, after all if you stay in this line of work for any length of time you will make quite a few enemies. I would sometimes sit in the car for a good five minutes to watch and wait for a while before I decided to get out. I always backed into the parking space as well so if you have to make a quick getaway it is much easier if the car is facing in the right direction; you just have to put your foot down and you're away. Why make it easy for them? It may sound a bit strange to some people or bordering on paranoia to go through such precautions. Well, I am here to tell my story. I know of at least two people who are no longer around and there are many others; maybe if they had varied their routine a little they may still be alive...

It's called survival.

I leave the car park and approach the club. I decided to go in through the beer garden which had tall surrounding walls and a high wooden gate, it was always locked so I jumped over the top and climbed down into the beer garden; now I could enter the club through the back of the conservatory. The reason being is that the fellas who are coming back to sort me out could already be inside possibly turning up before the lads had arrived on the front doors. The door to the conservatory wasn't locked, it never was, it was a little stiff though and so you had to give it a good shove in the right place to get it to open. I open the door and enter the club, it was virtually empty.

I ask the other two lads to work inside; I explained that I wanted to be on the front door all night. They thought it was a little strange but they knew it must have been for a good reason. I didn't want to get them involved in this one. So I told them nothing, what they don't know can't hurt them.

The rain was still falling adding to the already unpleasant nature of the evening. I wore a three-quarter length waterproof coat for obvious reasons also for concealment purposes; I must have looked like Blakey from *On the Buses*.

Right then, body armour on, bruising irons in place. Now it is just a matter of waiting and staying switched on. Cold and wet I stayed put in a position that gave a good all-round view for any attempted attack upon me. I hardly acknowledged the people rushing along through the rain. I was just concentrating on looking out for my would-be assailants. One thing about me was that I never forget a face; as soon as they appear I'll take the fight to them, bash them up and disappear… They never showed.

The art of war is simple enough. Find out where your enemy is.

Get him as soon as you can.

Strike him as hard as you can and as often as you can.

Ulysses S Grant.

I feel that at this particular point in time it was becoming easier to settle problems with violence or to resolve the arguments on the door with a right-hander and I wasn't too bothered about it either. You have got to be able to switch it on and off. I was finding it increasingly more difficult to switch off; the job does that to you after a while.

I was becoming the same as the violent idiots that I have been fighting against.

I didn't really need the job any more, my wife had gone back to work ages ago and I still had my day job so why am I still here? I've got nothing to stay for really. Is it through some form of misplaced loyalty...? To whom... I don't know? So what was it then?

Was it a bit of a power trip? I was the head doorman; the lads would carry out my instructions without question, if I said you are not coming in that was that, absolutely no argument about it. If I said you were leaving, out you would go one way or the other. The camaraderie was another thing. Sometimes it was just like a night out with a few pals; it didn't seem like you were at work. So there are aspects of the job which are agreeable. The nightlife and the lively music scene and the regular punters who were genuinely pleased to see you. I don't really have a clear answer. I knew it wouldn't be long before I turned it in though.

A few months on now and this weekend was to be my last. I had a feeling there was going to be a few problems. I don't know why but it seems that sometimes you can sense the *negative vibes* in the air.

The club was full of Welsh rugby supporters that had made the long journey down to London to watch their team take on the English at Twickenham. Right at the beginning of the evening we notice that three lads are involved in a bit of a scuffle at the bar, which was five deep with rugby fans. I had seen one of them before and I remembered he had a bit of an attitude problem the last time he was here.

I go in with Simon and calm the situation. The problem was being caused by a local self-styled hard nut; apparently he had been involved in some sort of altercation earlier on but we hadn't seen what had happened so we give him and his two mates the benefit of the doubt. We went back to the front doors keeping an eye on the three lads. As I look over towards the bar area the taller of the three gives one of the rugby supporters a punch in the side of the jaw. He goes to the floor and scrambles up to his feet and runs outside. Who does this geezer think he is? Once again Simon and I go in leaving the other two lads on the front doors, but it's a different attitude from us this time. You three are leaving, I say to them, they ignore what I say or they may not have heard me say it, owing to the noise. The taller one of the three punches a guy who is standing at the bar waiting to be served, right in front of us. This bloke's a bit of a nutter, I thought to myself. That old familiar adrenaline rush is making its presence felt big time. We both step in and a scuffle begins, the tall fella turns around and is about to throw his tried and tested right-hand punch at me. After a few of these types of confrontations sometimes you can anticipate what is about to happen and counter your attacker. After all I had just seen him throw two right-handers. My guess is he'll be throwing another one but you have to look for the signs, that's where your training comes in. I see his shoulder move back slightly, with his right hand cocked, he also carried his left very low. I move off to the right a fraction away from his right and deliver my own right-hander, which lands smack on the point of his chin. The blow knocks him backward four or five feet and onto a table, Simon drags him up to his feet. I say to Simon to get him around the neck and take him outside but he couldn't manage it the problem being that this guy is about six two and Simon is about five nine. I didn't want to move forward because I've got his two mates either side of me. I have them both in my peripheral vision; they are just waiting for the opportunity to do something the moment my back is turned. It's a bit of a balls up, where are the other two lads? My guess is that they can't see what is going on due to the crowds and no radios are in use here either (a communication breakdown). Meanwhile Simon and this fella are engaged in a scuffle, against my better judgement I go in to give him a hand. I had an idea what was going to happen so I was ready for them. As soon as I went forward one of them jumps on my back. That's it I've had enough of these people, they have clearly arrived here with one thing on their minds... trouble. They thought they could come here to bully, frighten and intimidate people. I grab the guy's arm which is around my neck and execute a really good judo throw on him. He goes right over my shoulder and for a moment I thought he was going to go through the large plate glass window that overlooked the high street. Luckily he lands on a table with a crash scattering and smashing the bottles and glasses as he lands. He must have knocked himself out because I didn't see him get up. This is all happening extremely fast, you understand; the other guy decides to have a go. He also jumps on my back and starts to strangle me from behind, he's not doing a bad job either. He had a really good grip around my neck. I could feel myself becoming light-headed and my vision was starting to fade out, in a matter of seconds I'll be going down and out to the floor. I manage to force my hand up the inside part of his elbow and grab the sleeve of his jacket and manage to swing him around in front of me where I deliver a hard jolting left upper cut to his jaw. It was an excellent punch; you know when you have delivered one just right. It had to be. If I hadn't landed that punch I would have gone down. I grab him by the hair and give him two more short sharp well-aimed left hooks to his chin. As I let go of his hair he falls to the floor unconscious where he gets the order of the boot. Actually I think the first punch had knocked him out and it was only by me holding him by his hair that was keeping him upright. One of the other lads is involved now and drags the fella out. I didn't have a clue what else had been happening but as I started to regain some form of normality I hear some very loud hysterical screaming. It was coming from one of the young barmaids, she was looking down at the floor where a crowd was now gathering. I look over and see the guy who Simon was scuffling with earlier lying flat on his back.

He was unconscious with blood covering virtually the whole of his face. I get a bit closer; and as I knelt down beside him I could hear that his breathing was very shallow, the music went off and the lights came on illuminating his face, which presented a horrible spectacle. His face was a red mask. With his lips turning blue I had to do something quickly. The blood from his injuries had run down into his throat which was slowly choking him. I remembered some basic first aid, the A B C, airway breathing and circulation. I tried to turn him on his side into the recovery position checking that he had not swallowed his tongue. I took hold of his head but it was so slippery with all the blood that I lost my grip and it slipped out of my hands and banged into the hard wooden floor with a sickening thud. I managed to get him into the recovery position; that seemed to do the trick. All the blood that was restricting his breathing was vomited out. His breathing started to return to normal but he was still unconscious. Police and ambulance arrived and he was taken away.

I asked the lads what had happened. Apparently Simon knocked the guy to the ground and then gave him a dozen or so unanswered blows to the face while he was out cold, how stupid is that? He could have died, and for what? We would *all* have been implicated.

I went into the gents' toilet to wash the blood off of my gloves and watched the water from the tap turning red as it spiralled its way down into the waste pipe; a few minutes ago it had been quite happily pumping around inside someone's veins. That's when I decided this was my last weekend on the door. A punch-up is one thing; this was out of order as far as I was concerned. I went back into the bar, the blood had been moped up, the DJ had started up again and the lights had been dimmed. People were drinking, dancing and enjoying themselves within a few minutes as if nothing had happened. I went back the next night and that was that. I had spoken to Pete earlier on the next day and told him that it was going to be my last night at the club. He came down later on that evening and at closing time we had our last nostalgic drink at the place.

The club closed down two months after my departure.

And so my journey into this strange and hazardous occupation has come to an end. What conclusions can I draw from the experience? I can't say I'm proud of anything except maybe the way I handled my fears and the way that I stood up to certain individuals. All I can say is that I genuinely tried to keep the decent people safe from the drug dealers, drunks, bullies and scumbags. We took all the crap so the genuine punter didn't have to and that's what the job is all about. At one point I did feel that the violence was taking over but I managed to suppress it successfully enough in the end without too much effort. The experience has changed my thoughts about some things and reinforced my opinions on other issues. The behaviour of people under the influence of drink and drugs was a real eye-opener. There are a few decent doormen out there with the same attitude as I had. In fact I know there are. Thin on the ground they may be but nevertheless they are there… It's a mug's game, and a fucking dangerous one as well.

GLOSSARY

Adam and Eve	believe
Acker Bilk	milk
biscuits and cheese	knees
basin of gravy	baby
Bruce Lees	keys
big dippers	slippers
bat and wickets	tickets
battle cruiser	boozer = pub
butchers	butcher's hook = look
bacon and eggs	legs
bonce	top of the head
bottle	courage
bricks and mortar	daughter
brown bread	dead
Cain and Abel	table
China plate	mate
Dicky bird	word
Donald Duck	luck
dustbin lids	kids
four by two	Jew
fourth of July	tie
ginger beer	queer
ginger ale	jail
Gregory Peck	neck
half inch	pinch
horse and cart	fart
Lady Godiva	fiver

loaf of bread	head – 'use your loaf'
mince pies	eyes
mud hut	gut
Nuremberg trials	piles
on your uppers	The soles of your shoes have worn away leaving only the upper part exposed = devoid of cash.
plates of meat	feet
pork pies	lies
rabbit and pork	talk
Roman candles	sandals
rub a dub	public house (pub)
septic tank	Yank
sky rocket	pocket
syrup of fig	wig
tea leaf	thief
Uncle Ned	bed
Vera Lynn	gin
wallies	idiots
S P	Starting prices at a race-course. What's the S P? = What's going on?

Printed in the United Kingdom
by Lightning Source UK Ltd.
108152UKS00001B/26